conquer picky eating

for teens and adults

---

activities and strategies
for selective eaters

JENNY MCGLOTHLIN MS, SLP AND KATJA ROWELL MD

ISBN-13: 978-1986385930

First Edition

Printed in the United States of America

© 2018 by Jenny McGlothlin and Katja Rowell

Published by Extreme Picky Eating Help
Dallas, TX

Book design by: Stephanie Larson

Edited by: Stephanie Larson

14 13 12 11 10 / 10 9 8 7 6 5 4 3 2 1

for parents

This book is intended for readers in late adolescence through adulthood. Appendix V in this book offers tips on how you can assist your teen or adult child on this journey. More resources are available at our website, www. extremepickyeatinghelp.com. Children are likely to do better with more parent guided/facilitated support; please refer to our book, *Helping Your Child with Extreme Picky Eating* (New Harbinger Publications, 2015) to learn more about how to help your younger child. It also provides a helpful foundation for understanding why your teen or adult child eats the way she does, and how you can help.

privacy

We have changed individual identifying details in the experiences and quotes shared by clients and others.

medical

This book and the information it contains are provided for educational purposes only. The text of this book is not intended to replace careful observation, evaluation, diagnosis, or ongoing medical or nutritional care as warranted. The text of this book should not be used in place of such careful observation, evaluation, diagnosis, or ongoing care. **If serious issues such as difficulty maintaining weight or weight loss are present, individualized professional care is of the utmost importance.** The authors have provided general information in this book and cannot make any assurances regarding the applicability of any information to any particular person in any particular set of circumstances. The reader assumes all risk of taking any action or making any decision based on the information contained in this book. The authors shall have no liability or responsibility for any such action taken or decision made by any reader of this book, and no liability for any loss, injury, damage, or impairment allegedly arising from the information provided in this book.

financial and conflict of interest

We receive no financial reward or incentive from any person or products mentioned in this book, other than royalties from our book, *Helping Your Child with Extreme Picky Eating* (New Harbinger Publications, 2015).

praise for *Conquer Picky Eating*

"This workbook offers respectful, validating, and empowering guidance for teens and adults who want to expand their eating on their own terms."

—Katherine Zavodni, MPH, RD, www.kznutrition.com

"A long overdue, step-by-step guide that actually helps teens and adults make peace with food."

—Skye Van Zetten, advocate and founder of Mealtime Hostage blog and online parent-peer support group for selective eating

"As a provider, this book is EVERYTHING I want my clients to learn! I can't wait for my clients to have a copy and to work through it together!"

—Erin VandenLangenberg, PhD, child psychologist specializing in eating disorders

"McGlothlin and Rowell have again created a wonderful resource for working with picky eating, but this time, directly for the eater themselves. In this unprecedented workbook, full of systematic, sequentially guided exercises, these wise authors cover everything from the mechanics of trying and learning to like new foods to recovering from the shame of not being adventurous with eating to enhancing self-acceptance, health, and overall well-being. Eaters will feel reassured and emboldened to find their path to more expansive eating, however they define that for themselves. This book fills a glaring gap in the self-help eating literature. I will recommend Conquer Picky Eating to many, many clients. Bravo!"

—Elizabeth Jackson, MS, RDN, LDN, specializing in eating disorders

"Jenny McGlothlin and Katja Rowell guide parents and young adults in navigating the value and significance of each person's trust journey with food. Their tips are practical, accessible and, best of all, rooted in the desire to foster an honest dialogue with our children and ourselves. This important book's easygoing style will support anyone to become a competent eater... a gift we all deserve in life."

—Carrie Lutter, LCSW, RD, www.carrielutter.com

"I absolutely love your new book. I appreciate that you celebrate each selective eater's uniqueness without judgment and that you offer hope with very practical, sensitive suggestions. You engage selective eaters as partners in the process of learning to enjoy their mealtime experiences."

—Marsha Dunn-Klein, MeD, OTR/L, co-author of *Prefeeding Skills* and creator of the Get Permission Approach

acknowledgments

First and foremost, we thank our clients for trusting, teaching and inspiring us.

We would like to thank the many colleagues and thought leaders in childhood feeding and adult eating who have guided us along the way. We have also included your information on our website resources page. Thank you to the writers and leaders in mental health; your work on attachment, trauma, anxiety, and depression informs everything we do.

We thank Katherine Zavodni, RD, MPH; Erin VandenLangenberg PhD; Elizabeth Jackson, MS, RDN, LDN; and Carrie Lutter, LCSW, RDN for their careful reading and feedback. In addition, Carrie provided welcome input on the nutrition and weight and health sections. You all helped make this a better book.

We offer a special thanks to Skye Van Zetten, the creator and administrator of Mealtime Hostage, a blog and private Facebook support group serving over 7,000 families (as this book goes to press). Skye's tireless volunteer advocacy has created and maintained a safe space for those dealing with extreme picky eating.

Last but not least, thank you to our husbands for their unending support and love, and our children for their patience, love, and the wonder and humor they bring into our lives.

table of contents

table of contents (cont.)

introduction

Chances are, if you're reading this book, you feel pretty discouraged about what and how you eat. You've probably been eating this way for most of your life. Our goal is to help you understand why you relate to food the way you do, offer tools to help you learn new skills, and:

- support your appetite
- decrease anxiety
- make peace with food
- learn to actually enjoy new foods
- enjoy the socializing that happens around food

What we know from adults who are "competent eaters" is that eating is most enjoyable, and nutrition improves, if you eat because *you want to.* This is known as *internal* motivation; discovering the desire to eat that comes from inside of *you.* This is eating that comes from being able to tune in to your body's signals that you need more fuel from food or hydration from drinks. Or perhaps you choose to eat because it brings you pleasure.

Eating tends to be less enjoyable when someone says you *should* eat or uses rewards or pressure—in other words, if you are eating for *external* reasons.

We'd like you to keep the following points in mind as you make your way through the book:

- Be kind to yourself on this journey of discovery. Sometimes the more pressure you put on yourself, the harder it will be.

- Give yourself permission *not* to try new foods if you're too anxious or don't feel ready. There will be plenty of opportunities. Other people forcing you to eat, or forcing yourself to eat (if you are upset or nervous) can backfire. You will learn why in the next few chapters.

- Try to have patience with the process. Some readers may make lots of progress quickly; for others, there will be steps forward and back. You might need to remain focused on one exercise for a period of time.

  The process of learning to tune in to your body's appetite and hunger signals and make peace with food will take time.

Worldwide research is ongoing on how to address selective eating (including picky eating, selective eating disorder, neophobia, and avoidant restrictive food intake disorder, or ARFID).

The content of this workbook is based on available research and advice from other experts in the field, and it is also supported by strategies that have helped our clients, friends, and readers.

> "Success" with eating looks different for different people. Some of you may turn into "foodies" down the road, others will learn to enjoy enough foods to eat out comfortably, and some might add a handful of foods to round out basic nutritional needs. Why not reach for the stars? You might not have to settle for slogging through meals or chasing every bite with a slurp of soda or a piece of candy, as you may have been told. For some, changing the eating experience from a negative to at least neutral (or not unpleasant) one may be enough.

how to use this book

This book is organized into separate chapters with brief explanations of key ideas. They follow four main themes:

- Understanding your eating

- Discovering and supporting your appetite, including the role played by anxiety

- Rehabilitating your relationship with food

- Learning to like new foods

These ideas and thought exercises are meant to help deepen your understanding and allow you to gain insight into your eating challenges. Exploring the reasons for the ways you relate to food will help you move forward and recognize they're not your fault. We don't want to overwhelm you with information, statistics, and research, so we summarize explanations and try to keep the exercises short and to the point. Take them one at a time, spending as long as you need on any given topic.

When you reach the end of a chapter, go back and read the full chapter and your notes in one sitting to reinforce what you learned.

This book will provide enough ideas and inspiration for some readers to have huge breakthroughs and feel satisfied with their progress. For others, progress may feel slow and even discouraging. Some of you may go through this book with a therapist or need to find other professional help (see Chapter 40). You might put the book away for a few weeks, then come back to it. You might repeat an exercise or look back and reflect on how far you have come. We recommend using a supplemental "journal," which can be a simple spiral notebook or an app such as Stream Journal to flesh out some of your observations and experiences.

There are different paths toward making peace with food, many of which we will explore through the exercises in this book.

For more resources, check out https://www.extremepickyeating.com/teenadultresources.

For a few words of encouragement, read this letter from Skye Van Zetten, advocate and founder of Mealtime Hostage blog and online parent-peer support group.

Dear Reader:

The exercises in this book are intended for teens and adults who have diets that are limited to a short list of foods because of preferences for taste, texture, and temperature. It might surprise you to know that most people have preferences and dislikes for food, and that you, like everyone else, are entitled to the privilege of discovering what foods you like and don't like on your own terms.

You've arrived at a place where you believe something about your eating needs to change. Maybe you feel the food you can eat isn't good enough or your food choices could be healthier. Maybe you want to feel more confident about the food you choose to eat in the company of friends. Maybe you're worried about how the food you find safe and appealing will affect your future. Whatever your reasons for holding this book in your hands, know you are not the only person in the world who feels this way. You are not alone, and I know you're not alone because I've heard from hundreds of teens and adults, and I have spoken to thousands of parents around the world who want for their children the same thing you want for yourself: a healthy relationship with food.

Here, in your hands, are pages of hope. Hope is a place in the future where anything seems possible, but before we explore this hopeful future place, let's spend some time understanding the most important part of your journey with food. Before the first step of any journey, there is always a reason to exchange what is known in the present for the unknown adventures of the future. Obviously, you seek change, which is already a huge accomplishment! (Congratulations!) What I want to know is this: what is it about your eating that inspires you to make it different?

Every journey needs a beginning.

I'll let you in on a little secret. The most common response from parents to this question is, "I want my son/daughter to eat vegetables so they'll be healthy." Maybe you've heard something similar from your own family or significant other? It's good to have goals; however, the question is not about where you want to go, but why you want to change. Don't worry if you aren't sure. It's not an easy question to answer.

The strange truth is that often, parents of younger, non-vegetable eating children learn their children are ALREADY healthy, and eating vegetables won't make them noticeably "healthier." Nothing against vegetables, but there are other food groups that also play nicely with others. As a parent, I have been told more times than I can count that children SHOULD eat vegetables, even though vegetables tend to be among the most challenging foods to like. Wrapping vegetables in "shoulds" does little to improve their flavor.

"Shoulds" are some of the most physically and mentally noxious dietary substances anyone ever insisted you ingest. I can tell you from personal experience that any food—from any food group—tastes so much better without a dusting of "shoulds" and when you believe it will be enjoyable to eat.

*So... What is it about your eating now that inspires you to make it different? I can suggest any number of possibilities, but, I encourage you to come up with your own answer. Your reasons might still be full of future goals and "shoulds" that you've heard from other people over your entire life. Keep searching for your own personal motivation, because this journey is not about anyone else but you. **This is your journey.***

As you work through the exercises in this book, you may find that what motivates you to explore food and new food experiences may change as you become more comfortable with food selection. Your reasons for selecting the food you choose to enjoy are your own. Trust yourself, from this moment forward, to eat to the best of your eating ability, and know that your best is enough.

You've got this!

Skye Van Zetten

Why we use the terms "selective" and "picky:" You may think of yourself as "picky" or have been called "picky" by others. This word can feel more like a condescending label than a simple description of your eating, and it can become part of your identity. To some, it implies being bratty or refusing to eat certain foods on a whim. "Selective" can be a more respectful word to describe eating patterns that may be limited due to preferences in taste or texture, or for a variety of other reasons. You will notice we do occasionally use the word "picky" in this book and online because it is a common word, many adults and teens identify themselves as such, and we want others to find help through online searches.

Every exercise or tip in this book is an invitation to explore things that might help. If any exercise is very difficult, makes things worse, or is upsetting, that is useful information; it may point you to an area where you need more help or possibly professional guidance.

Let's begin!

1
understand selective eating

Everyone wants to feel comfortable and safe when eating. Uncomfortable, difficult, or painful experiences *while learning to eat* make it harder for children to develop a trusting relationship with food. This kind of history often plays a role in **extreme selective, or "picky," eating—that is, not eating enough variety or quantity to the point that it impacts your physical health, your social or emotional well-being (if eating causes you significant stress or worry), or your ability to interact with family or others in your community.**

The following are some common reasons why people avoid or dislike eating (now or in their past):

"It hurts:" Medical issues, including reflux, constipation, and allergies or food intolerance, link pain and discomfort with eating.

"I don't want to:" Being told to do something as personal as eating by an authority figure (such as a doctor, parent, or boss) can push a person in the opposite direction. Throw in a history of anxiety and scary experiences around food, and over time this resistance—"I won't (or can't) like it!" can become automatic, even for foods not yet tried.

"I can't:" If tongue, cheek, or jaw muscles were weak or not working properly while a person was learning to eat, scary incidents can result, such as choking or having foods or liquids go down the airway. Individuals born prematurely or with other developmental delays are also at higher risk. Jaw misalignment or other structural differences also affect the experience of eating.

"I don't like how it feels:" Being highly sensitive to certain textures, smells, or flavors (which is more common with sensory problems or for those on the autism spectrum) can make eating unpleasant.

> Being sensitive or having sensory challenges describes a way of experiencing the input from the world around you. For some, that input can feel too intense—as if everything is turned up too much. This can lead to difficulties with crowds or loud noises, intense irritation with seams in clothing or certain fabrics, or the inability to handle bright or flashing lights. People who experience the world this way are often described as sensory "avoiders" who may try to "turn down" the intensity of input.
>
> Others seem to have difficulty *picking up* sensory input, as if everything is turned down so low they can't sense it. This might describe sensory "seekers" who seek to "turn up" input.

These ways of experiencing the world play out in relation to food, which we will explore in later chapters. Sensory seekers may prefer spices and crunchy textures (more input), whereas sensory avoiders may prefer bland foods and avoid intense flavor or textures.

Consider the categories in the following table. **Circle** any factors or symptoms you think may apply to you. Which one or two categories have the most items that describe you?

I don't like it (sensory)	It hurts (medical)	I can't (oral motor)	I don't want to (temperament, past challenges)
Certain textures bother me	I have/had food allergies or sensitivities	I have/had medical or surgical issues that affect/ed eating	I was forced to eat certain foods and didn't like it
I only eat foods that are soft or don't take much chewing	I have/had frequent ear or throat infections	I had or suspect I have a tongue tie*	I am strong-willed and hate to give in or give up
Smells are a big problem for me	I have/had chronic or severe constipation	I was born prematurely	I want to do things my way on my time
I won't eat mixed textures, such as noodles in soup, or stews	I have/had mouth or tooth pain	I have/had orthodontic devices that limit movement	I prefer to struggle and figure things out rather than have help
I need lots of crunch or spicy foods	I have/had major medical problems or surgeries	My mouth gets tired when I chew tough foods*	I've had negative experiences (gagging/ vomiting) when eating
I prefer bland, room-temperature foods	I have/had acid reflux or heartburn	I have trouble keeping liquids/food in my mouth while eating; people tell me I eat like a kid	I don't like new things and new situations/I like things to be the same

*If you have trouble chewing or moving foods around in your mouth, talk to your dentist or seek an evaluation with a speech-language pathologist. We occasionally see teens and adults with problems that were missed during childhood. An apparently rare condition, known as PANS (pediatric acute-onset neuropsychiatric syndrome), can present prior to puberty with sudden onset of extreme picky eating, often with obsessive thoughts or fear of choking (without an inciting choking event). It can be triggered by an infection or, in the case of PANDAS (pediatric acute-onset neuropsychiatric disorders associated with strep infections), specifically streptococcal infections.

Refusing food or being selective was potentially a way to maintain a feeling of safety and comfort. Those behaviors at one time may have made sense and served you well. **It's not your fault you are picky. You're not being lazy or stubborn, as you may have been accused in the past. Eating is complicated!**

Maybe you *didn't* have any of the above underlying challenges and were just a typically picky child. About half of children are picky, but most grow out of it. Perhaps you were especially strong-willed and independent. If you were rarely offered different foods for any number of reasons or were allowed to make peanut butter sandwiches every night for dinner, that lack of opportunity could have also led to persistent picky eating.

Other possible factors contributing to picky eating:

- **Having picky parents;** picky parents are more likely to have picky children. There appears to be a genetic component.

- **Being a "supertaster,"** which is a person who has more taste buds than average and experiences tastes more intensely than others, especially certain bitter tastes. This trait occurs in about one in four people and may be more common in picky eaters.

- **Getting less pleasure from eating** ("If I could just take a pill and never eat again, I'd be fine with that.") About one in four people have *fewer* than average taste buds, which researchers have labeled "non-taster." We wonder if getting *less* flavor or input from food helps explain why some people seem less interested in eating, or may prefer highly salted or spiced foods.

- **Having medical challenges or taking medications** that impact appetite or taste.

The next several exercises suggest bringing your parents in for some extra history. **Don't worry if you aren't comfortable bringing your parents into this process. It may not feel good or safe to ask them these questions right now, or you may not have parents to ask.** That's okay. You don't have to talk to your parents to reflect on your early eating development. Parents do the best they can. For some of you, that best was not consistently good. Anything that gets in the way of a parent's ability to respond sensitively to their children means the children's basic needs are not likely to be met. If you grew up in a home with addiction or mental illness, or where you did not always feel safe and loved, that impacts your stress level, appetite, and how you learned to relate to food.

If you don't have supportive parents or family, that can feel tough. Hang in there. Don't skip questions about early feeding. Write down your impressions, fill in what you can, and keep going. Siblings may also be able to fill in some of the gaps. This is just the beginning. You can also skip this chapter and come back later.

You'll start to notice a theme throughout the book: **you are in control, this is your process, and do what works for you.** After you've worked through most of this book, Chapter 39 will help you write a letter to family and friends if you want to share this process with them and ask for more help and understanding.

◆

If you feel comfortable doing so, ask your parents to look at the categories and factors contributing to picky eating on page two with you. Ask if they have any memories of your early experiences around food or can provide medical history that you might not know about. What did you learn?

_____

_____

_____

_____

Babies often explore the world through their mouths; the tongue and lips are highly sensitive. That's why parents "baby proof" the house—everything goes in the mouth! Ask your parents if they remember whether you mouthed objects or not. Not mouthing may be a clue there was a problem early on.

_____

Ask your parents if *they* were picky as children. If they were and no longer are, when did it change and why? If a parent still eats limited foods and has strong food preferences, ask if they can explain why they don't like certain foods.

_____

_____

_____

If you have siblings, they may eat very differently from you, even though they were raised by the same parents and offered the same foods! Maybe a sibling jumps into new experiences while you like to observe first, take your time, and be more cautious or independent. Think about your sibling(s) and review the list again. How are you and your sibling(s) different?

_____

_____

_____

How are you similar to your sibling(s)?

_____

_____

How did your parents/caretakers respond to any similarities and differences?

_____

_____

_____

2
what "normal" eating looks like

"Normal" eating depends a lot on the culture and time in which you live, as well as available resources such as money, foods, food storage, and preparation. In some countries, it may be the norm to either eat one large meal, or several small meals, throughout the day. Entire cultures and groups of people have survived over centuries on very limited choices. The Inuit near the Arctic Circle traditionally ate mostly caribou, raw seal, whale, and fish (not many leafy greens there!) and in parts of Britain, even into the 1970s, garlic and pasta were seen as exotic.

> There is no one right way to eat. Knowing that many happy and healthy people eat very differently can help you make peace with how you eat now, freeing you to make changes that feel good to you.

Observe and reflect: List the people in your family or others who are close to you and note their eating traits and preferences. For example, what words come to mind when you think about how they eat? Do they eat fast or slow, lean toward spicy or plain foods, or prefer meat or fruits? Do some family members seem to get more pleasure from eating or planning meals than others? Who forgets to eat? Who gets "hangry" (moody with hunger)? Who is dieting or has dieted in the past? Who sits down to eat and who eats mostly on the run? Who has a "sweet tooth" and who prefers salty foods?

Name: _____ Eating traits and preferences: _____

_____

_____

Name: _____ Eating traits and preferences: _____

_____

_____

Name: _____ Eating traits and preferences: _____

_____

_____

Name: _____ Eating traits and preferences: _____

_____

Name: _____ Eating traits and preferences: _____

_____

If you feel comfortable, ask your family members how they feel about their eating. See if your observations match up with their impressions of themselves. What did you learn?

_____

_____

_____

_____

If anyone in your family is or was a picky eater, ask them about that experience. Did your grandparents eat mostly the same foods as children, such as potatoes, boiled veggies, and meat? Did they eat foods particular to their heritage only or enjoy cuisines from different cultures? Did they enjoy kiwis, avocados, or other imported items? Did they remember times when they did not have enough food to eat or food felt scarce? One teen was surprised to learn that her grandmother didn't have access to an orange until she was eight years old, and that she drank only reconstituted powdered milk or water growing up.

_____

_____

_____

_____

Childhood experiences impact eating into adulthood, including how adults then feed their own children. Research tells us that children who grow up without enough food on a reliable basis, known as "food insecurity," have increased focus on food; increased rates of binge eating, hiding, and hoarding food; and other challenges. Many who have experienced food insecurity find it *very hard* to see food go to waste and may be more likely to pressure children to "finish their plates" or take a few more bites.

Do any of the people in your family or close circle eat in a way you wish you could? Who is a "good" eater? Which of their habits and values do you admire?

_____

_____

_____

What does it mean to you to be a "good" eater? What might be "good enough?"

_____

_____

_____

_____

notes

3

explore your early relationship with food

How we relate to food starts on day one of life with those first feedings of breast milk or formula. The relationship continues with that first spoonful of rice cereal, pureed peaches, or green beans. If things go well, as babies we learn to trust that we will be fed—and trust our parents to pay attention to our inborn hunger and fullness cues around feeding. We continue to expand our food experiences as older babies and into toddlerhood and preschool. By the time we are school-age children, we trust the signals coming from our bodies about how much and what kinds of food to eat.

Mealtimes can, and ideally should, be pleasant for families. However, for many of you, problems likely started early. **Early childhood challenges or struggles around eating and mealtimes often play a role in persistent selective eating. The early "feeding relationship" (what happened around food between you and your parents or the people feeding you), helped shape how you relate to food.**

To review, anything that may have made drinking or eating painful, uncomfortable, scary, or unpleasant, understandably increased the odds of avoiding (or feeling anxious around) eating. And guess who was trying to figure all this out when you were a child? Your parents! One of their main jobs was to feed you to facilitate growth and development. Even if your parents asked for help, they often got bad advice. Many *doctors* don't even know how to help. Odds are your parents did the best they could with the information they had.

Serving a variety of tasty foods at regular times and eating together as a family helps children grow up to eat well, but that doesn't always happen in our modern world. Often, parents have worries that impact how they feed. The three most common things parents worry about are: 1) their children are not eating *enough*, or the "right" foods; 2) their children aren't gaining weight or growing fast enough; and 3) their children are eating too much of the "wrong" foods and are gaining too quickly. These concerns understandably lead many parents to try to *get* children to eat more or different foods. Pressuring kids to eat has been strongly linked to kids eating *less*, preference for high-fat and energy-dense foods (think packaged and fast foods), and eating fewer fruits and vegetables. **Often, the more parents worry, the harder they try to get kids to eat, and the worse things become.** Understanding how your relationship with food started will help you make peace with food.

◆

Parents often learn how to be parents from their own childhood experiences. Ask your parents what mealtimes were like *for them* as children. What were the rules? Did they have to eat everything on their plates? Did they enjoy mealtimes? If they were picky, when did they learn to like new foods? Did they wish anything was different *for them* as children around mealtimes?

_____

_____

_____

_____

Look at your baby pictures together. Did they worry you were too small or didn't eat enough? Did you have trouble with bottle or breast feeding?

_____

_____

Was there a time when they thought you ate well?

_____

_____

What do they remember about mealtimes with you when you were little? What do you remember?

_____

_____

_____

_____

Did you have regular mealtimes? Did you sit at a table or eat in front of a TV, smartphone, or tablet?

_____

Did you have regular snack times, such as after school, or did you eat when and what you wanted?

_____

Did you prefer to eat in the car, on the go? At a friend or relative's home?

_____

_____

Were you regularly given your accepted foods while your parents ate different foods or at different times?

_____

_____

Circle any strategies your parents or others used to entice you to eat more or different foods over the years:

bribes

rewards (including toys, cash, stickers, etc.)

negative consequences (losing screen time, etc.)

nutrition discussion

encouragement or praise

threats

comparison to a sibling or friend

preparation of special foods

having you help cook

putting you on a diet

other _____

_____

_____

Did you ever participate in any feeding therapies or psychology appointments to address your eating? If so, what do you remember? Did it help? Did it make things worse?

_____

_____

_____

_____

Do any experiences stand out as especially scary or embarrassing? Were you ever forced or coerced to eat? Did you ever vomit at the table or in public? Did you ever gag or feel sick while eating with others? Did you ever feel shamed or threatened?

_____

_____

_____

_____

_____

Many therapy approaches and therapists recommend various ways of making children try and swallow foods. These experiences are scary for many children. If this happened to you, know that your parents were likely told this was the best option and were desperate to help you.

   If you ever have flashbacks or nightmares about eating or past events around food, you may be experiencing a trauma reaction. The following could have triggered your fight/flight/freeze responses: being forced to eat; being held down or feeling a lack of control; or having gagging, choking, or vomiting episodes that were frightening or when you couldn't breathe. If that sounds true for you, or if you are triggered by any of the exercises in the book, please find professional help with someone trained to work with trauma. Even if you don't remember exactly what happened, you can still have that response. Body-focused therapies such as yoga, dance, and embodied therapies may prove healing for you.

If someone tried to get you to eat something, how did you feel?

_____

_____

_____

_____

Was there any technique that worked to entice you to try *and like* new foods or get you to eat *one* bite of a food, but not more? Was the experience pleasant or unpleasant?

_____

_____

_____

_____

_____

_____

_____

_____

Trust and feeding are intertwined with your relationship with your parents. What feelings and reflections come up around your childhood memories of food and mealtimes? **Circle** any of the following that complete the statement, "I felt . . . "

confused	sad	coerced
annoyed	ignored	like no one believed I could do it
cared for	cherished	like it was no big deal
angry	not listened to	like I got a lot of attention
hurt	overpowered	

other _____

_____

Can you share this list with your parents? _____ Friends? _____

◆

Express yourself in a way that feels comfortable to you: journaling; writing a poem, song, or blog post; or venting to a trusted friend, school counselor, or therapist.

◆

Food-for-thought experiment for friends and family: Ask them to name a food they find utterly disgusting. If they can't come up with any, name a nonfood item that won't hurt them, such as dirt or a beetle. Ask them what reward or incentive would get them to eat it: being allowed to eat a favored food afterward, or perhaps $5, $10, or even $1,000? Explaining that selective eaters feel the same way about many or most foods can help others understand what you go through at mealtimes. It also points out how useless bribes and rewards are in most cases. Understanding and imagining themselves in your shoes, even briefly, can make a big difference in others. Keep in mind, however, that this technique might not work with the rare person who enjoys eating any and all weird things!

notes

4
mealtimes past and future

A shared mealtime is about much more than food; it is a time and place to connect with family and friends. For some, memories of past mealtimes are pleasant; for others, they are not. Did you enjoy company at mealtimes but always ate macaroni? Or perhaps there were a variety of foods you could eat, but you were reminded often to eat. Possibly, the nagging, battles, and tears are what you remember most.

> A few exercises throughout the book ask you to draw or color. The act of creating art uses different parts of your brain that opens the door to new ideas and discoveries. Don't worry about your artistic abilities—it's not about how pretty the picture looks.

Draw a picture representing your family meals when you were little. Who is saying what? Use speech bubbles if you like. Label who is at the table. What colors do you think of? Color in the people, speech bubbles, and shapes or shading that might describe the mood at the table.

Draw a picture of your *ideal* family meal and use speech bubbles to write down the words you would like to hear. What colors do you imagine or associate with pleasant mealtimes?

If drawing isn't your thing, create a "wish list" of your ideal family meal. Who is there? What are you eating? What are you talking about?

_____

_____

_____

_____

What were snack times like for you as a child? Were you alone after school? Were the foods different? Were snack times easier or more pleasant than meals?

_____

_____

_____

If you have positive memories of snack time, can you list a few reasons why snacks went better than meals?

_____

_____

_____

Now imagine eating with a young child, such as a relative or neighbor (or maybe even yourself when you were younger). What might you talk about? What if they didn't want to eat something at the table? What would you say to them?

_____

_____

_____

_____

notes

5
understand anxiety, appetite, and hunger

Selective eaters experience eating and mealtimes differently; some feel little or no desire to eat, while others feel hunger and look forward to eating, but are intimidated by certain foods. Some selective eaters avoid eating with others and feel embarrassed or anxious about their eating, which can cause stomach upset and dampened appetite—a vicious cycle. **Emotions, appetite, and digestion are all connected. Exploring how you experience eating, physically and emotionally, will help you tune in to and respond with kindness to your body's cues.**

> **hunger:** a: a craving or urgent need for food or a specific nutrient b: an uneasy sensation occasioned by the lack of food. (*Merriam Webster online*) We think of this as mostly physical sensations arising from a need for fuel.
> **appetite:** a natural desire to satisfy a bodily need, especially for food. (*Google Dictionary*) We tend to think of appetite as hunger combined with the desire to eat, largely due to pleasure experienced while eating.
> **full:** satisfied, especially with food or drink. (*Merriam Webster online*)

The mechanisms controlling hunger and appetite are incredibly complex and not fully understood. Among other factors, there are chemical messengers called hormones that go from your brain to your gut and back, special "stretch" sensors in your stomach that help you know when you are full, and one crazy vagus nerve that connects your brain, heart, and intestines! The vagus nerve is sometimes responsible for nausea or a clammy or lightheaded feeling and can speed or slow your gut movements (digestion), resulting in diarrhea or constipation. We're also learning more about the role of the billions of bacteria in our intestines.

> Taking probiotics or eating yogurt or kefir with live active bacteria may help restore healthy gut bacteria, which can help regulate digestion. Talk to your doctor if you are dealing with long-term or severe constipation with infrequent, painful, or hard bowel movements. Your doctor might help you choose a fiber supplement or a stool softener.

Anxiety is common for selective eaters, so we will cover anxiety more thoroughly than other emotions. Anxiety might come from a past scary or uncomfortable experience with food, anticipation that you won't like a food, or concern that someone will make you eat or drink something. Feelings aren't just in your head; they are expressed and experienced in your body, such as a tight feeling in your stomach or tension in your shoulders.

There are no wrong emotions. It's important to learn to recognize feelings that might get in the way of a healthy relationship with food. **When you explore where emotions come from and why, you can begin to deal with them, tune in to your appetite, and learn to relate to food in a new, healthier way.**

◆

In this exercise, you will **explore your reactions to different foods** *without other people around.*

Start by sitting in front of a few different but familiar foods. Using the lists below, **check** which emotions or physical sensations come up; these will provide clues to your emotional state. At first it might be hard for you to recognize your emotions, but the more you practice and cue in to your emotions and physical sensations, the easier it will become.

emotions

_____ anxiety	_____ nervousness	_____ unease
_____ disgust	_____ upset	_____ agitation
_____ hopelessness	_____ hope	_____ distress
_____ curiosity	_____ worry	_____ content
_____ apathy ("whatever")	_____ concern	_____ other _____

physical sensations

_____ gagging	_____ shakiness	_____ headache
_____ nausea	_____ queasiness	_____ neck pressure or shoulder tightness
_____ vomiting	_____ disconnection	_____ stomach cramping or dull ache
_____ fatigue	_____ hollow	_____ numbness or tingling in fingers or feet
_____ sweaty palms	_____ dry mouth	_____ pressure or tight feeling in chest/stomach
_____ clammy	_____ rapid breathing	_____ urge to go to the bathroom
_____ rapid heartbeat	_____ dull pressure	_____ achy
_____ tension	_____ sharp pressure	

_____ other _____

What happens when you put foods in front of you that you don't like or don't want to eat? Go through the list again.

_____

_____

_____

Were there any surprises or connections you hadn't made before?

_____

_____

Review the lists of emotions and physical sensations several times in the next few days. What reactions do you notice when *only new* foods are provided?

_____

_____

_____

Why do you think that is?

_____

_____

_____

What do you feel when new foods are presented alongside a food you regularly eat?

_____

_____

_____

Do you react differently depending on how hungry you are?

_____

_____

On this outline of a body, use pens or colored pencils to draw or color in what you feel in different areas of your body when you feel stressed about food or eating.

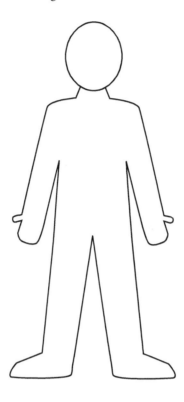

While you are focusing on feelings and sensations, the next time you experience something before, during, or around mealtimes or food, **pause and pay attention.** Perhaps close your eyes so you can notice what is going on in your body. Don't judge a sensation as good or bad, or try to stop or change anything.

Describe what you feel. Sit with the sensations; take deep breaths. Is the sensation round? Sharp? Hollow? Heavy? Dull?

_____

_____

_____

If you simply allow yourself to feel, how do the sensations change after a few minutes, if at all?

_____

_____

_____

6
explore eating with others

Now that you have begun to explore your inner experiences around new and familiar foods, we invite you to shift the focus of your attention to the outside world. You may have discovered that when there is no expectation or pressure to eat certain foods, they didn't bring about much of a reaction from you, or maybe they did. **Negative feelings can also come from what you know, or imagine you know, about what other people think about your eating. Fear of judgment or being shamed, and wanting to eat to please others when you cannot, can make peaceful mealtimes hard to achieve.**

◆

Eating plays a big part in our social lives, and a sense of belonging is a vital human need. List three times in the last week or two that social outings or gatherings focused or centered on food.

How were those experiences for you?

1. _____

2. _____

3. _____

At some point, you have almost certainly heard comments about your eating from those around you. Judgment may come from friends, family, colleagues, teachers, physicians, and even commercials! Social media makes us even more aware of judgmental attitudes. You may feel vulnerable to criticism, which can lead to a sense of isolation and avoiding eating with others. Let's think about how shame, embarrassment, or wanting to fit in impacts how you feel and how those feelings can interfere with, or sabotage, signals of hunger and fullness coming from your body.

◆

Who has labeled you or described you as "picky" or "selective?" Write down their names and what they have said: (parents, doctors, classmates, friends, etc.)

_____

_____

_____

What do you feel you miss out on or avoid because of how you eat?

_____

_____

_____

_____

What words do you use to describe your own eating? **Circle** some and add your own:

embarrassed	don't care	whatever
it's fine	it's not important…	no big deal
failure	"I'm picky"	empowered
babyish	I don't like it	can't be bothered
picky	I can't like that	don't understand what all the fuss is about
loser	I can't	

other _____

Look back at the list of sensation and emotion words on page 20. Think about how you feel while eating, depending on who is with you. Did you circle different words if you were eating alone, alone with a screen, or with your parents versus a trusted friend?

_____

_____

_____

_____

check in

When you finish a chapter, have you remembered to read through it with any notes? Reviewing what you've learned will help these new ideas replace unhelpful patterns.

7

take stock of what you eat now

You're early into this process. Take a snapshot of your food experience right now. Take some time to fill in the food preferences list at the back of this book, in Appendix I. We also have the table available as a PDF on our website under the resources section for this book if you want to print it out. Reflect on and fill in the lists under the columns for foods you eat now and enjoy, foods you eat now but don't enjoy, foods you ate in the past but do not eat now, foods you are interested in trying, and foods you can't imagine eating. There is also a place to list your accepted sauces and condiments, etc. You may want to ask your parents which foods you ate when you were younger. Hang on to this list for later exercises as you begin to think about characteristics of foods, how to branch out to new foods, and which ones to start with. You may want to write this in pencil, so you can come back and make adjustments, or take notes every few weeks or months and see what changes.

Seventeen-year-old Thomas filled in his list of foods when he began working with Jenny to address his selective eating. He has eaten the same eight foods for as long as he can remember: mint chocolate Clif bars, fried chicken tenders from a few different restaurants, French fries, Doritos, peeled apple slices, dry toast, chocolate chip cookies, and plain spaghetti noodles. He occasionally enjoys ketchup with his French fries and has tried marinara sauce before and didn't hate it. His mother frequently tells him he ate many more foods as a toddler and has even shown him pictures of him happily eating spaghetti with meat sauce (with a sauce-covered face to prove it). Thomas listed his eight foods under the "eats and enjoys" list and ketchup as his accepted condiment. He put marinara sauce under "used to eat but do not eat now," and his mother helped him fill in the rest of the foods in that category.

Describe the experience of filling in the food preferences list.

_____

_____

_____

_____

Were there any foods you listed that you had forgotten about? Did you experience a sense of surprise or excitement about maybe eating any of these foods again?

_____

_____

_____

notes

_____

_____

_____

_____

_____

_____

_____

_____

_____

_____

_____

_____

8

accept how and what you eat now

We get it; you're reading this book because you want to change your eating. But change is likely to come more quickly if you can begin to accept how and what you eat now. Bear with us as we explain.

A major source of anxiety can be the pressure you put on yourself to eat a certain way. You have explored how other people pressuring you to eat may have made you more resistant. As we grow up, we often internalize the words of others. So instead of our parents, the doctor, or our favorite celebrity telling us we "should" eat something, we beat ourselves up (self-talk) or feel badly if we aren't able to eat those foods yet. You might even feel shame, guilt, or agitation when you have thoughts such as, "I should be able to eat some grilled chicken…" Over time, those messages feel like the "truth," and expectations follow. It can feel strange to think that addressing the pressure you put on yourself, and *accepting how you eat now*, is a critical step to reducing anxiety and resistance.

Acceptance is a common theme in many therapies, including acceptance commitment therapy (ACT); dialectical behavioral therapy (DBT), where it is even called "radical" acceptance; and motivational interviewing. The idea is that struggling against the selective eating is worse than the actual selective eating and its consequences. **Like quicksand, the more you struggle, the worse off and more stuck you become. Acceptance means not getting stuck in negative feelings about how or what you eat. This doesn't mean giving up if you don't want to; it means giving up the shame and blame. Doing so allows you to be more open and curious and take advantage of opportunities. We believe you can and will learn to tune in to your appetite and you can and will learn to expand what you eat when you are ready.**

> *"When I changed my thinking from 'I have to eat this' to thoughts of curiosity, like, 'I wonder what that tastes like,' I slowly felt more open to trying new things."*

Identify negative thoughts around eating when they come up. List some of the negative self-talk that intrudes on a regular basis.

_____

_____

_____

Visualize each negative thought and judgment like it's a hot potato—and drop it. Another option: notice the thought, then sweep it away—you might even make a sweeping motion with your hand.

Rewire your brain! Ban the word "should" and come up with some new self-talk. Every day for the next three days, say three new, positive phrases out loud three times and write them out by hand. Set an alert on your phone to remind you to say whatever phrases fit you the best. Look at your daily schedule to determine when you might need a boost in confidence, when you seem to feel the worst during your day, and right before you go to a social event featuring food. You could pick one phrase as your ready-to-go "mantra" that gives you a sense of confidence and calm as you face challenges.

Circle three of the phrases below or write your own.

"I can do this! I'm learning about foods."

"I will learn to like new foods when I am ready."

"My way, on my time."

"This is my journey and I am in control."

"I'm curious about what I will notice today."

"Every meal is a fresh start."

"I am not defined by what or how I eat."

_____

_____

_____

> You will see the focus is on shifting your attitude to **curiosity**, being on a **journey**, and **discovery**—not on how many bites you eat.

Can you think of or look up other inspiring phrases? Song lyrics? Lines from a poem or religious text?

_____

_____

Here are some gentle ways to frame your experiences around food that also give you permission to explore at your own pace. See which of these phrases works for you:

"I might…"

"I discovered I prefer X because it is…"

"Maybe I will…"

"I don't like it yet."

"I may or may not like this someday, and that's okay."

"Next time I could…"

"That was unexpected."

"I wonder what would happen if…"

"That smells different."

"I didn't like it when I was three years old."

"That's a new taste for me."

> At first these phrases will feel "fake," but repeated over and over, they can become your new truth. Or put another way, "fake it 'til you make it."

Try the alerts and reminders for three days (and as long as you want) to change the internal conversation. How does it feel?

_____

_____

_____

Continue to combat counterproductive, automatic thinking patterns. Another helpful phrase acknowledges that even when you experience anxiety, it does not take over *all* of you, and you still have inner reserves of calm strength you can draw upon. Try saying, "*Part* of me is feeling anxious," or "*Part* of me is curious" about unknowns, such as how that sauce would taste, if it would taste better heated up, or if it might taste good with a cracker.

Try using the phrase, "**Part of me feels**…" over the next few days. How does it feel?

_____

_____

_____

◆

Be patient. You may have felt badly for a long time about how and what you eat. These patterns don't change overnight. It will take practice to challenge those automatic thoughts and replace them with new ones before you really begin to believe it.

notes

9

figure out what sabotages your appetite, hunger, and confidence

Many things can undermine your eating, such as anxiety, certain flavors or smells, comments, certain people, eating or drinking small amounts throughout the day (grazing), or stress. What affects one person negatively may have no impact on someone else.

> Kai was helping his Dad make pasta sauce one day and noted that it smelled good. He and his dad were excited, and he even tasted, and liked, some of the sauce from the pot while it was cooking. Kai sat down to the meal and Dad poured a big spoonful of sauce onto Kai's pasta. Kai felt his pulse quicken and his hunger disappear. After reflecting, he found that the large portion made him anxious because he felt pressured to finish it. Kai had discovered that having others serve him, and facing large portions, put him off. Kai came up with ideas to try the next time, such as using a small bowl to start, serving himself, or even dipping pasta (rotini works well) into the sauce.

As you consider your past meals and snacks (also known as *eating opportunities*, or EOs), **which of these situations below decreases your appetite or made you anxious around food? Check all that apply:**

_____ large portions

_____ pressure to eat or try food

_____ people watching me eat

_____ music (loud or soft)

_____ people watching and not eating with me

_____ distracting noise

_____ negative comments from others

_____ TV or screen

_____ praise from others, of me or the food

_____ worry about future health

_____ food touching

_____ what might be hiding in my food

_____ what other people might think

_____ tense conversations

_____ eating food that is different from what others are eating

_____ distracting pets or people

_____ colorful plates

_____ certain colors

_____ certain smells or flavors

other _____

_____

Eating Opportunity **(EO)** is another way of saying "meals and snacks," as a reminder that food is food—there aren't necessarily different foods for meal and snack times. EO also stresses these are *opportunities* to explore new foods, pay attention to and satisfy hunger and appetite, and fuel the body.

Reflect on your experiences around meals and food. Two evenings this week, after your last EO, review the list on the previous page and write down anything that negatively impacted your eating. Consider how you might gain some control over each item you wrote down, such as serving yourself smaller portions if larger portions put you off, or reducing distractions. Note that upcoming chapters will help you deal with many of the listed factors that can sabotage eating.

_____

_____

_____

notes

_____

_____

_____

_____

_____

_____

_____

_____

_____

10
support your eating

Food stylists spend hours making a meal look as enticing as possible for magazines, cookbooks, TV shows, and commercials. Many factors can make food look or seem more appealing: the name of the dish, lighting, background music, restaurant decor, color of food, or how food is presented. Many restaurants serve food with a visual garnish (such as a sprig of parsley) or additional flavor enhancers (such as a lemon wedge or a pickle) that aren't listed on the menu.

The previous chapter focused more on things that make your eating worse, which are often easier to identify and avoid, than on figuring out what *supports* your eating. Some situations, scenarios, people, and even times of the day can enhance appetite and hunger and support your journey toward making peace with food. This activity will assist you in discovering what helps you do better with eating—in essence, what makes food more appealing to you. These might take the form of the company you eat with, the background music, or even a favorite plate.

◆

Think about a time when you tried a new food or felt open or curious. Then answer the following questions:

Where were you at the time? _____

Were you there to eat (mealtime), or did food just happen to be around? _____

Who were you with, if anyone? _____

What time, or meal (breakfast, lunch, dinner) was it? _____

What kind of mood were you in? _____

What were you talking about or doing? _____

Describe another time when you added a new food to your accepted food repertoire. Are there similarities to the previous scenario? Is there a pattern?

_____

_____

If you can't remember such a time, can you imagine a pleasant eating opportunity (EO) when you come to the table calm and ready to eat? Close your eyes and imagine that experience. If possible, envision a room or other setting that feels comfortable and safe, and answer the following questions:

How is the lighting? _____

Are there people with you? _____ Who are they? _____

_____

Is there music? _____ If so, what kind? _____

What kind of silverware is available? _____

What kind of plates are there? _____ Placemats? _____

Are you on a chair or bench? Are your legs dangling, or are you sitting with a leg tucked under you, such as on a picnic blanket?

_____

Other ideas?

_____

_____

> Aliyah notices she eats the most at breakfast. She figures the reason is because she hasn't eaten in over eight hours, plus with her roommate getting ready for work and rushing out the door, she doesn't sense as much attention on her eating. The time of day and the people who are with her make a big difference in Aliyah's appetite.

Over the next several days, if you have an EO or an encounter with food that *feels good*—or at least not *bad*, if that is where you are at right now—write down what is happening. Pause and pay attention. Include as much detail using as many of your senses as you can. What do you hear? Smell? See? Touch? And finally, taste?

_____

_____

_____

11

learn who you are— apart from your eating

When you struggle with something—eating, anxiety about school, a learning disability, a job, you name it (please do!)—it can feel as if that is *who you are*. You might think "I'm the picky eater" or "I'm the anxious one." You may have been labeled "picky" for as long as you can remember. And, because we eat many times a day and much of our social life and culture revolves around food, it can feel as if how or what you eat defines you. *It doesn't.*

> You are not defined by what or how much you eat. You are a unique individual, with many wonderful qualities and quirks.

You aren't what or how much you eat. Taking time to think about and celebrate what makes you unique, seek what makes you happy, or discover a cause you feel passionate about can help you *focus less* on your eating. When you aren't focusing on all that is *wrong* with your relationship with food, you can approach food with a more open mind, and your appetite and curiosity around new eating experiences is likely to improve.

Your eating has resulted in some positive outcomes; you have grown and nourished your body and mind to do the amazing things you do. Focusing on what you do *well*, putting positive energy into things you enjoy, and recognizing that your eating can get better with time can reduce anxiety and boost your confidence. Even though this exercise isn't directly about eating, it's still important.

◆

Circle words you could you use to describe yourself:

funny	independent	calm in a crisis	playful
curious	stubborn	hardworking	a volunteer
smart	a good friend	a team player	an animal lover
generous	stylish	loyal	an artist
sassy	confident	reliable	musical
athletic	organized	studious	
thoughtful	creative	ambitious	

other:_____

Circle activities you enjoy or that you are good at:

listening	teaching things	reading	doodling
math	taking care of kids	meeting deadlines	my job
debate team	art	crosswords	computers
empathizing	making music	singing	doing thoughtful things
helping others	dancing	puzzles	for friends and family

other: _____

What are your goals (that have nothing to do with food) and dreams for the future?

For next week? _____

_____

For next year? _____

_____

Ten years from now? _____

_____

◆

If you aren't sure what you are good at, or what you like to do, **consider finding time to volunteer for a cause on a regular basis.** You could walk dogs at a shelter, take on a weekly shift for Meals on Wheels, or read to children at an after-school program. For opportunities in your area, check out www.volunteermatch.org or search online. People who volunteer and practice compassion for others tend to be happier and less anxious.

Sometimes your eating may be a focus of attention from those around you. **See if you can come up with things you enjoy doing with family or friends that have nothing to do with food:** watching a movie, hiking or biking together, or checking out a new coffee shop or gallery. Consider asking someone close to you if you can schedule a fun or enjoyable activity, or just time to hang out once a week. Get to know each other while keeping food out of the equation.

List three activity options you could do with others that don't involve food:

_____   _____

_____

12
set goals for eating and mealtimes

Many selective eaters avoid eating with others because they are embarrassed or are tired of unwanted comments and judgment. These feelings of shame (I *am* bad or wrong, versus guilt, which is the feeling you *did* something bad) can get in the way of improving your eating as well as limit social connections. Being purposeful and clear about your goals can help banish shame and open the door for moving forward.

social goals

What would you like to accomplish or experience when eating with others? Write down three goals:

1. _____

2. _____

3. _____

food goals

What are your short-term goals (in the next few days or weeks) around the kinds and amounts of foods you would like to investigate? Write down three goals:

1. _____

2. _____

3. _____

long-term goals

What are your long-term goals (six to 12 months down the road) around the kinds and amounts of foods you would like to eat or the kinds of social experiences you would like to have? Write down three or more goals:

1. _____

2. _____

3. _____

4. _____

5. _____

> Make a collage about your eating and your goals. Cut out pictures from magazines, make a Pinterest board, find clip art, or draw pictures of food or situations that line up with your goals.

Sometimes, after years of thinking you "should" eat more fruits and vegetables, coming up with different goals feels confusing. If you felt stuck trying to come up with goals, consider the following ideas. **Add any items that spark your imagination to your goals lists on the previous page.**

- feeling comfortable eating with others

- being okay with ordering only bread or fries

- focusing on enjoying the company of others instead of fretting over what I will or won't eat

- learning to eat chicken, as it's on most menus

- enjoying a new food or a food I like prepared in a new way

- expanding the variety of crackers I can eat

- adding one new fruit per month

- learning to not be put off by food others are eating

- avoiding thinking and worrying about food so much

notes

_____

_____

_____

13
reclaim "healthy"

Our culture is obsessed with what and how people eat. So-called experts promise good health if you eat "super foods" such as chia seeds and kale or avoid other foods such as dairy and gluten; the list is ever changing. Maybe a coach or employer is challenging you to avoid sugar or eat more protein. It seems we can't get away from nutrition advice and lectures, and you may not realize that the benefits of vegetables and certain ways of eating are often exaggerated. In reality, how nutrition impacts your health is a lot more complicated than eating like a caveman or drinking green smoothies. You aren't just what you eat. Selective eating is rarely an emergency. **"Health" means a lot of things, not just not being sick. If you are focused only on the health benefits of vegetables, for example, you miss important opportunities to actually improve your health.**

When "healthy" eating is bad for you: Some people who eat only the "healthiest" foods are in fact struggling. While not considered an official eating disorder, "orthorexia" is a highly problematic way of eating in which the worry and rules around eating only "healthy" or "clean" foods and avoiding "unhealthy" foods dominates a person's life. Orthorexia is characterized by intense anxiety, which makes people feel worse rather than better. The National Eating Disorder Association describes orthorexia this way: "…food choices become so restrictive, in both variety and calories, that health suffers—an ironic twist for a person so completely dedicated to healthy eating. Eventually, the obsession with healthy eating can crowd out other activities and interests, impair relationships, and become physically dangerous" (www.nationaleatingdisorders.org/orthorexia-nervosa, accessed 2018). You may have friends, family, coaches, co-workers, or health providers who think they eat well but are in fact struggling with disordered eating.

This exercise is about discovering things you can do to help you feel better now and enjoy better health— that have nothing to do with your eating. The following is a list of factors linked with improved health and wellness. You don't have control over all of these factors, but you may already enjoy the health benefits of many of these.

Put check marks next to any items that you do or that apply to you:

_____ owning a pet   _____ having health insurance

_____ moving my body   _____ having a stable financial situation

_____ getting outside in nature   _____ not being discriminated against or bullied

_____ practicing meditation, relaxation, or yoga   _____ having people in my life whom I love and who
                                                  love me

_____ having a "purpose"
                                            _____ belonging to a religious or spiritual community
_____ helping others
                                            _____ practicing gratitude and compassion for myself
_____ not smoking   and others

Look at the following lists of health-promoting behaviors. **Circle** one item from each list and schedule them in your calendar at least twice this week. Pay attention to how you feel before and after each activity.

social and emotional health

- do something for someone else such as holding a door open or taking out the trash

- volunteer

- attend a religious service or pray

- meditate

- call a friend

- text a funny video or joke to a friend

- sign up for a good-news feed or funny animal videos

- practice gratitude, jot down what you are grateful for every day or use Gratitude Journal app

- write a letter to someone who means a lot to you

- practice random acts of kindness such as giving a thank-you card to a restaurant server, favorite teacher, or volunteer

- talk to a neighbor, aunt or uncle, teacher, or school counselor whom you get along with

- sketch something at the park that catches your eye: a door, a design in the brick, or a pretty flower

- hang out with a friend (see Chapters 21, 22 and 39 on how to help your friends understand your challenges so they can help you)

physical health (move your body in joyful, satisfying ways)

- try a yoga class in person or online

- walk to school/work/around the block

- go to the dog park with your dog or borrow a neighbor's dog

- learn karate

- learn Tai Chi

- stretch

- dance to some tunes

- play catch with a sibling or friend

- join an Ultimate Frisbee or Disc golf league

- swim

- hike

- bike

- reduce and manage stress (see Chapter 20)

- other _____

self-care

Remember to eat, drink, stand up, take deep breaths, get ready for bed, and take any necessary medications. If you often "forget" to eat or go hours without eating, you may need to schedule these activities. You can use reminder alerts on your phone or computer or find a self-care app such as Perspective Daily Journal or Aloe Bud. (Be careful not to let reminders to "eat healthy" throw you. You are redefining what that means for you.)

Don't forget about sleep: Teens and young adults are notorious for not getting enough sleep, and it impacts anxiety, appetite, and routine.

How many hours of sleep do you average right now? _____

Do you catch up on sleep on weekends? _____

See if you can get to bed even 15 minutes earlier each evening. Try to go to bed around the same time most nights and wake up around the same time most mornings, avoid screens for an hour before bed, and watch your caffeine intake and timing. Americansleepassociation.org has additional tips for getting more sleep.

notes

14
learn a new food language

The way you think about food, or that voice inside your head, matters. Right now your vocabulary around food may be limited to general adjectives such as gross, slimy, okay, or yucky. Are you able to explain what *specifically* you don't or do like about certain foods? This chapter includes exercises to help you explore language around foods, expand your vocabulary, and begin to change your inner voice.

◆

Watch a cooking show or two, listening carefully, and write down any descriptors they use. Are they specific to properties of the food, as in "salty, crunchy, sweet," or general adjectives that could describe other things, such as "beautiful, amazing, delicious?"

_____

_____

_____

Now review the list and **circle** words that stand out in a good way. Put an X through words that are less appealing.

Refer to your food preferences list in Appendix I to consider "foods you eat regularly." What characteristics do they have? Think in terms of flavor, texture, color, temperature. Choose three foods from this list and describe them.

Texture examples: crunchy, soft, wet, dry, crumbly, chewy, sticks together, creamy, pasty

Flavor examples: savory, sweet, spicy, salty, cinnamon, vanilla, sour, chocolaty, fruity

food: _____ characteristics _____

food: _____ characteristics _____

food: _____ characteristics _____

food: _____ characteristics _____

food: _____ characteristics _____

Using your food preferences list, look at your list of foods in the "eat now and enjoy" column (if you don't "enjoy" any foods right now, think of this category as "eat regularly") and think about their flavors and textures. Do you notice any characteristics shared by those foods? Do any food adjectives show up more than others?

_____

_____

Using your food preferences list, think about foods you have eaten in the past but don't eat now. Choose a few and write them here.

_____

_____

Why do you think you stopped eating them? What about them did you not like in terms of taste, texture, flavor or color? Were there other factors playing a role in your dislike?

_____

_____

_____

Choose one or two specific foods to explore that you have eaten in the past but don't eat now. Pick ones you have at home or can easily access; what do they look, smell, or feel like? Describe them. Taste them only if you want to.

_____

_____

_____

Do your memories match the characteristics of the food in front of you?

_____

_____

_____

15
make foods familiar

Now that you have increased your language around foods, actually exploring them will be a bit less intimidating, and you will get more out of the process. *Familiar* things become less scary. (This can also be called "exposures," but you are in control.) The following are a few ideas for first-step exposures. You already watched cooking shows in the last chapter, and that's part of the process too!

◆

Watch videos of animals eating, such as hamsters eating tiny burritos (Google it, we think you'll like it), or a fruit bat eating a banana. If moist foods are unappealing, sometimes watching a cute animal lick and gnaw on a banana is a good way to get used to the idea before you can handle the person next to you eating it, or perhaps yourself!

Explore with senses other than taste. Find out if a new food is sweet, salty, or crunchy. How can you explore food without eating it? Ask others to describe it for you with specific words. Read the label, looking for descriptor words. Look for hints about texture before you touch it. Try smashing the food inside a plastic baggie or between wax paper (don't have to touch or smell it directly) with your fingers, a rolling pin, or a fork. Then smell it. You could touch it to your lip and lick your lips, or touch it to a fork and put the fork in your mouth.

Write down your impressions after each step.

_____

_____

_____

_____

Find what *looks* good. Go to a bookstore or library and browse cookbooks or cooking magazines. Don't feel you have to buy any; just look at the pictures. Cookbooks for children may be a great place to start. These often have fewer ingredients and may have less complex flavors. Or scroll through Pinterest, starting with a food you like, such as sugar cookies or French toast. Browse for 10 minutes.

What appeals to you? Colors? Foods from cultures other than your own?

_____

_____

_____

_____

Are you drawn to certain ingredients or food groups? Maybe breads or fruits?

_____

_____

_____

Did you enjoy looking at certain kinds of foods more than others, such as an appetizer section more than casseroles?

_____

_____

_____

How did looking at the cookbooks and recipes make you feel?

_____

_____

_____

Watch a few different kinds of cooking shows. A competition show with a focus on food _and_ some distracting drama might be fun. What kinds of foods or techniques caught your eye? What was not appealing?

_____

_____

_____

_____

check in

From Chapter 9, review the checklist of things that might dampen or kill your appetite or decrease pleasure at mealtimes. Think about the last few days. Did you experience anything (social, food, etc.) that made your eating feel worse to you?

_____

_____

_____

Were you able to identify what was happening at the time?

_____

_____

Take a moment to reflect on any meal or snack that has gone well in the last few days. Have you made any observations about what supports your appetite or helps your eating?

_____

_____

_____

_____

_____

_____

_____

notes

16
improve your nutrition now

It will likely take time for you to heal your relationship with food and learn to enjoy a wider variety of foods. In the meantime, you can improve your nutrition with the foods you do eat, in creative ways. Remember, you are not a test tube. Some days you might get a bit more of a nutrient, such as protein, and some days a bit less. You might begin thinking about nutrition in terms of a pattern of intake over several days. (Please see Appendix IV for details on protein and other nutrients.)

◆

Don't forget about fruit. Many selective eaters have a few fruits they enjoy, or one or two more nutrient-dense foods such as peanut butter or yogurt. If there are fruits you enjoy, be sure to include them often throughout the day. **Fruits have many of the same nutrients as vegetables, including fiber and vitamins.** They are not inferior to vegetables.

Write down any fruits, including canned, frozen, freeze-dried, juiced, or fresh, that you enjoy.

_____

_____

_____

Smoothies can be a great way to include options. If you enjoy yogurt or cold drinks, you might try experimenting with smoothies. They don't have to be green! Try a smoothie blended with milk or yogurt, almond or soy milk, or your favorite juice or ice cream. Add a small piece of frozen banana or frozen fruit and blend well. If seeds bother you, start with seedless fruits. Experiment with adding different fruits and start with small amounts. You can also freeze the smoothie into pops. If you're not ready yet, skip adding new foods. You will get acquainted with new foods in later exercises.

Add fruits or veggies to baked goods you already like, if that feels okay to you. Recipes abound online for adding blueberries, zucchini, black beans, or spinach to brownies or muffins, for example, and can be quite good. You can ask a friend or family member to make them for you if you prefer. Be sure that no one "sneaks" veggies, fruits, or supplements into your food! If this has happened to you in the past, you may have felt tricked or betrayed, or maybe you didn't notice and then were teased. As long as *you* are in control, though, you can use some of those food "sneaking" recipes and books.

Look into supplements. You may be getting enough of certain vitamins if you eat fortified foods such as cereal, crackers, or dairy products. Many selective eaters don't get enough DHA (an essential fatty acid). Consider chewable or gummy kids' vitamins, or if you can swallow pills, try adult DHA supplements. If you are a young woman and you don't eat meat or other sources of iron, ask your doctor to test your iron and recommend supplements if it is low. (See Appendix IV for iron information.) Low iron is not uncommon and can dampen appetite!

Sometimes if you eat a lot of fortified foods and take a multivitamin, however, you could get too much of a good thing. Talk to your doctor if you are unsure. You might benefit from seeing a registered dietitian (RD) or a newer designation, a registered dietitian nutritionist (RDN), who can help you target supplements. Work with an RD or RDN if your food options are so limited that you regularly drink—or think you need—liquid supplement beverages. If you rely on protein/meal bars or drinks such as Ensure for most of your intake, see if you can start to eat or drink them at regular mealtimes. See Chapter 25 for establishing a routine.

Chances are if you eat or drink one or two protein sources a few times a day, you get enough. Milk is a good source of protein, as are cheeses, meats, and nut butters. If you truly are low on protein and eat no meats, nuts, or soy products, look for protein-added foods such as bread, milk, cereals, pasta, and even protein powders to add to smoothies, pancake batter, or other foods. Consider working with an RD or RDN for advice. For more on protein, check out Appendix IV. You may find you are doing better than you think!

Explore more nutrient-dense versions of foods you enjoy. Can you try "whole grain" Ritz, Club Crackers, or Goldfish? What about white bread with added fiber or protein? Juices with added calcium or protein? Pasta with added fiber, protein, or DHA? Can you try the "Greek" version of a yogurt you already like to boost protein? With some foods, you won't notice any difference, or it won't matter, whereas with other foods, you might see a big difference in your enjoyment. Whole wheat tortillas, for example, often have a very different texture than white flour tortillas. Note: In general, we don't consider "low fat" to be healthier.

Go to the store or look online to see if there are any options for foods you eat regularly. List them. Consider trying one this week.

_____

_____

_____

If you think you have a food intolerance or allergy, keep track of the foods you eat and any symptoms. Sometimes symptoms are caused by other factors, including anxiety. Consider working through this book before eliminating any foods. Perhaps cut out caffeine or switch to lactose-free milk. If you are thinking of eliminating any foods, it is important to work with an RD or RDN to ensure you don't further limit your options and nutrition.

17
when you worry about food "waste"

Many people have a hard time throwing out food. You may have been scolded as a child to finish your food or to think of people who didn't have enough food (as if you eating the food on your plate would feed the hungry). Sometimes this tactic is used to guilt children into eating. With all the much-needed attention on the environment, wasting food or purchasing certain types of foods may bother you, especially if you don't know if they will get eaten. Consider putting aside these worries for now while you focus on your progress. It is better to work on these valid concerns when you have built some skills and feel more ready to deal with them.

Giving yourself the chance to try foods is not wasting. Reframe it. Giving yourself total permission to buy, prepare, and put food on your plate that you *don't eat* is not only okay, it is often a critical part of the process of learning to eat those foods. Preparing, shopping, touching, smelling, looking at, and passing a dish are all useful opportunities to get to know food. If you are "shy" with your relationship with new foods, it will take time to warm up. As you gain more skills around eating and preparing food, there will naturally be less waste.

Say to yourself: *"I am giving myself the opportunity to explore and try these foods."*

Consider sharing uneaten food with a family member, neighbor, or friend who knows about your journey with food. If you buy a package of cookies but decide you only want one or two, share the rest of the package at work, or buy a "snack" pack to start.

When eating out, visit restaurants with buffets. This way you can eat your favorites and get a separate plate for small samples of new foods to explore without the negative feelings associated with wasting food.

check in

Look back at the lists of health-promoting behaviors in Chapter 13. What items did you choose?

_____

How did it feel, and did you continue with those activities?

_____

_____

If not, why? _____

_____

Chose two more items from the lists and put them in your calendar for the upcoming week. What did you pick? Which days did you choose?

activity: _____ dates: _____

activity: _____ dates: _____

Put a reminder in your calendar to review those lists every two weeks so you can try out new behaviors and see what you have been adding to your life. Which activities were fun and felt good, and how can you make time to continue caring for yourself?

notes

_____

_____

_____

_____

_____

_____

_____

_____

_____

_____

_____

18
learn what makes your anxiety worse

Anxiety is quite common for selective eaters. Underlying anxiety or anxious tendencies can make you uneasy around food, which is made worse by constant pressure to eat. Sometimes it is hard to know which came first: Did the anxiety fuel the neophobia (fear of new foods) and the desire for familiarity, or did the constant attention and pushing leading to anxiety—or a mix of both?

> Obsessive compulsive disorder (OCD) is also linked with selective eating. If you notice tendencies to obsess, feel compulsions around foods, ritualize food selection, count bites, or avoid/eat certain foods because you believe you can cause or prevent something from happening, you may need to find professional help.

Becoming familiar with the sources of your anxiety is critical. Like many other teens and adults, you might struggle with body image, worry about college, or be anxious about work. Some people feel anxious when they are really hungry or in social situations. If the vague, anxious feelings can be traced to the source, perhaps you can do something about your worries, from addressing others' interference to working on your body image (see our online resources at www.extremepickyeating.com/teenadultresources). You've already begun to explore how you experience anxiety in various situations, so let's now go one step further and identify your main concerns.

> Anxiety decreases appetite and curiosity. Learning to gauge your anxiety will also help you identify triggers and learn ways to feel more calm and centered.

Go back and review the physical signs of anxiety on page 20 to help you tune in to and listen to messages coming from your body. When you experience physical sensations associated with anxiety, your body is trying to let you know something needs your attention and care. What are you anxious about, on a scale of 1-10? (1 = none; 10 = so severe you can't function, as in a panic attack.)

_____ your health or health worries

_____ past experiences

_____ how you look

_____ money

_____ school or work pressure

_____ the experience of a food

_____ social pressure or embarrassment

_____ fear you might choke on a food or vomit

_____ conflict with family or friends

_____ social media drama or feeling inadequate compared to friends' online lives

Are there things not listed on the previous page that you worry about?

_____

_____

◆

Getting in touch with your level of anxiety can help you know when it's a good time to explore a new food. If you're very worked up about something such as a test or conflict at work, you might feel less inclined to try something new. Identifying the sources of your anxiety empowers you to do something about it.

> If you previously ate in a typical way without problems, then had a choking or vomiting episode that triggered your selective eating, please find professional help. If you are limiting your foods and intake as a result of being afraid you will choke or vomit again, this often improves with therapy, especially if you catch it early. You may have emetophobia (fear of vomiting) or phagophobia (fear of swallowing).

notes

_____

_____

_____

_____

_____

_____

_____

_____

19

challenge your assumptions and control your story

Some therapies, such as cognitive behavioral therapies, help reduce anxiety by using your rational-thinking brain and skills. Naming what you are afraid of is a good place to start. You've done some of that already.

The trap of "all-or-nothing" thinking can fuel your fears: "I will *never* get better at this." "I *know* if I try that I *will* vomit" (when it hasn't happened in months or years). "*No one else eats like this*; there is *no hope*." "I fail at *everything*, and will fail this too." All-or-nothing thinking is a problem, but it also creates an opportunity to change for the better.

If you find you are stuck or overwhelmed with feelings of doom or worst-case scenario thinking, or you feel trapped in your negative thoughts, seek professional help.

◆

In a moment of calm, reflect on and write down your worst-case scenarios. What is the worst you are concerned might happen?

_____

_____

How likely is that to happen? _____

When did it last happen, if ever? _____

What is more likely to happen?

_____

_____

What has happened in the past?

_____

_____

Rewrite your worrisome scenarios with a positive outcome.

_____

_____

_____

_____

example

Instead of: "If I try this, I will gag."

Try: "I might try this and think it isn't so bad." "I might lick that piece of watermelon and not gag." "I might gag, but it will be over quickly, and I have this glass of water to drink if that happens."

Note: exercises later in this book provide ideas for dealing with nausea, anxiety, gagging, and how to try new things.

◆

What could you do to help make success more likely?

_____

_____

example

Instead of: "If I change my smoothie, it will taste bad."

Try: "When I make my smoothie, I'll put in one blueberry and see if I even notice it is in there."

Other ideas?

_____

_____

_____

Online support groups or forums for selective or picky eaters are a mixed bag. Proceed with caution. It can be very comforting to find a supportive group or person who understands your situation. Unfortunately, perusing comments in online groups can leave readers feeling hopeless if the focus of the discussion is venting over awful parts of others' situations. It's like asking a depressed person to feel better by reading only depressing stories. Ask yourself an important question: "How do I feel during and after being online with that person or group?" Hopeful? More calm? Or do you see no way forward? When in doubt, tune them out.

Two resources we trust are the Mealtime Hostage Blog (see their section on teens and adults at www.mealtimehostage.com) and the Mealtime Hostage private support group on Facebook (www.facebook/groups/mealtimehostage).

notes

20
manage anxiety and relieve stress

Every human being experiences anxiety, but too much of it—and in situations that aren't actually dangerous—is unpleasant and an obstacle to making progress with eating. Acceptance is often the first step in reducing anxiety, so you are on your way. Knowing and avoiding triggers helps, but you can also do a lot to decrease stress and access healing within your body.

Your parasympathetic nervous system is the counterbalance to your body's "fight-or-flight" responses such as a racing heart and tight stomach. Many of the exercises below strengthen the parasympathetic nervous system, making you more resilient to stress. **Anxious patterns take a long time to develop, and so does resilience. Just like with any activity or exercise, though, it will get easier, and you will enjoy more benefits if you practice these techniques regularly.**

◆

Access tools and resources you already use. Do you ever feel anxious or experience negative emotions at times other than eating? Perhaps before a big test or stressful work deadline? List ways you reassure yourself then.

_____

_____

_____

The following options (some are backed by research, and none should make things worse) explore decreasing stress and increasing confidence. You may find that a walk with soothing music works best, or deep breaths before meals. Play around with these, find a few that work, and stick with them.

relax

Choose three strategies and try them for 5-15 minutes before meals or when you need it most. Continue your favorite every day, and explore some you haven't tried.

_____ **Guided relaxation or imagery.** There are many free or paid apps including Calm, Breathe, Headspace, and Insight Timer.

_____ **Woodchopper yoga pose.** Stand with your legs about shoulder-length apart. Put your arms together in front of you like you are holding an axe. As you breathe in, lift your arms over your head and look toward the ceiling. As you breathe out, swing your arms and upper body down and breathe out through your mouth with a "Haaa" sound. Your head and arms may even swing between your legs. Then as you breathe in again, raise your arms above your head and repeat three to five times.

_____ **Breathing.** There are many variations of breathing exercises. Find one that feels good to you:

- Take 10 deep breaths in and out.

- Breathe in, hold it, and then give a big sigh and repeat three times—make as much noise as you want to.

- Count to four while breathing in, hold for four, and count to four while breathing out.

_____ **Binaural music** has specially timed rhythms and beats meant to help relax and synchronize brain-wave activity. There are both free and paid apps with music. This technique works best with headphones.

_____ **Biofeedback, such as with the "Heartmath" app and heart rate monitor.** The monitor clips to the ear and works with cell phones and tablets. This technique uses guided deep breathing to synchronize breath and heart rate variability. Earn points and rewards while relaxing.

_____ **Put your open hand over your heart area and press gently.** Close your eyes and leave your hand there for several seconds. See what happens to your level of anxiety.

_____ **Pray or lean on your faith and religious community,** if you have one.

_____ **Color** in a coloring book, do a puzzle, draw or doodle, make a mandala, or use an app such as Recolor.

_____ **More ideas:** listen to uplifting music, go for a walk, swing on a swing, jump rope.

What are some ideas of your own?

_____

_____

_____

_____

release

_____ **Write it down.** Write down what you are feeling right now about eating, or choose a time before a meal or a new experience with food. Don't judge it or try to change it. Just write it down on a separate slip of paper. Then ball it up, take three deep breaths and throw it away.

_____ **Journal for 15 minutes a day** for three days in a row about how you are feeling and any strategies that helped.

_____ **De-clutter your room and living space.** If an item doesn't improve your mood, let it go. Sometimes chaotic surroundings can be unsettling. Set aside an afternoon to clear out your car, your bedroom, etc. Toss and tidy. Showcase a few favorite photos, put up a poster you love, and take down ones that don't bring you joy anymore. Donate, recycle, and clear out. Get some new organizing containers to tame papers or bills. Put your laundry into a hamper rather than the floor. See if it improves your mood.

boost confidence

Excitement and anxiety can feel similar in your body, with a racing heart or sweaty palms. Anxiety tends to have a negative association, meaning you would rather avoid what is provoking the reaction. Try changing the thinking to *excitement,* which is usually associated with a positive outcome. Changing your language and frame of mind may make trying a new food more appealing.

_____ **Say, "I'm excited!"** three times before new exercises or challenging situations, instead of "I'm scared!" What are you "excited" about? To be out with friends? To be at a new restaurant? To read about new foods? To try a new food?

_____

_____

_____ **Strike a pose.** Standing tall, as though you're featured on a poster for the latest superhero movie, boosts confidence.

_____ **Listen to music with a strong, thumping bass beat.** Tap or dance to the beat, stomp or jump to the beat, pump your fist.

_____ **Take control of your story and write your own happy ending.** Some research shows that your narrative, or how you frame your experiences, can be empowering. More formal narrative therapy, done with a trained therapist, can be very healing. Reflect on your new understanding as to why you may be picky. Try to find a positive angle. Below is an example.

"I was born early and had lots of medical procedures. I survived that and grew up in spite of that hard beginning, which proves I'm strong. My early experiences with food weren't easy. My parents were scared and kept me alive and loved me. My body protected me from pain. Now I am learning to let go of that fear that served me as a child, but doesn't help anymore. I am happier, less controlled by my fear, and confident that someday I will eat well and take care of my body and spirit in lots of different ways."

Sometimes even when you use your tools, your stress level may remain high. It is okay to lean more on your accepted foods or feel less adventurous around food when there are increased stressors in your life. This is why people talk about "comfort foods"—everyone has them! Approach yourself with kindness and patience when stress flares. If you feel as though the stress or anxiety never gets out of the high zone, you probably need more help; talk to your doctor, religious leader, parent, or school counselor.

notes

_____

_____

_____

_____

_____

_____

_____

_____

_____

_____

_____

_____

_____

21
find your "eating support" people

This chapter is about recruiting a friend or family member to be an eating-support person, or helping someone who is almost there to be even better. This person or persons can support you in different ways: as emotional support, a non-pressuring companion at eating times, or a "discovery partner" who participates in the process more actively, such as helping you plan out meals and brainstorm new foods or sauces to try, be with you during mindful eating activities (Chapter 31), and be a sounding board for your observations. You may want a person who will provide occasional encouragement, while at other times, you may just need company. You might want more of a cheerleader type, and that's okay too. The important thing is having someone you trust who will listen to you.

Eating with someone who understands what you are going through, and who will accept you as you are can be a huge relief. Being "brave" feels easier with a friend or loved one, whether it involves bungee jumping, riding a roller coaster, going to your first school dance, or exploring a new town. Eating is no different. Having one or more "safe" people to eat with may be critical for you. Just as emotional support animals help with anxiety, finding your "eating support person" can be a huge help (and if eating with your dog works for you, go for it)!

> Friends can be a source of support but also of pain. Comments or "jokes" from a friend can really sting. Talking about this issue can leave you feeling vulnerable. Consider, "I know it seems like a joke, but this is hard for me, and it really bothers me when you tease me about what I eat." Try to have these conversations when you're not around food. See Chapters 21 and 39 for more on asking for help from friends and loved ones, and Chapter 22 on setting boundaries.

If you have a romantic partner who can be there for you on this journey in helpful ways, that's a bonus, but don't panic if they don't get it. Hopefully, if a significant other can't actively support this process, at least they won't tease or belittle you and will give you some space while you work on your relationship with food.

Sometimes the people we are closest to (our family members or romantic partner) are not able to be our eating support person. That can be hard, and you may have some grief to process around this. In some relationships, you may need to make adjustments or set boundaries around safe topics of conversation and find new ways to communicate in order to have your needs met as well as theirs.

What is important to you in a support person? List qualities. Examples: funny, kind, nonjudgmental, etc.

_____

_____

_____

Come up with two or three people who may be able to fill this role.

_____   _____

_____

Once you have identified someone, ask to meet them (not over a meal) or talk on the phone. Meeting in person may help them read your expressions and body language. Try not to approach them through text or email, where meaning is often misinterpreted. Write down the name of the person you will approach first and set a deadline, say a week from now, to contact them.

Who will I reach out to? _____

When will I reach out? _____

◆

Review the earlier exercises in Chapters 9 and 10 to be clear about what hurts and what helps your appetite and anxiety. You don't have to share any of your history with your support person, but if you think it would help, you can.

Have a discussion with your potential support person to introduce the idea.

The following are some sample scripts:

- "I learned my picky eating had a lot to do with things that didn't go well when I was a kid. I had (sensory, medical, pressured feeding, etc.) and mealtimes were scary and painful, so I learned to avoid eating in order to protect myself. I know it's hard to understand."

- "I'm not really sure why I eat the way I do, but I know my anxiety plays a huge part."

- "Here is what would really help me if you are willing…"

- "Do you think you might be able to help?"

- "Could you sit with me and keep me company, but not comment about what we eat?"

- "I could really use some encouragement when I try something new."

What else is important for you to communicate?

_____

_____

_____

◆

Pat yourself on the back for having the nerve to ask. If you don't feel confident that the first person you approached is the right person, pick another person, and try again. Asking for help can be hard. We are proud of you for trying. You don't have to have a support person who gets it, and you can do well if you aren't able to find someone. We hope this book will help you feel less alone in this process!

How did it go?

_____

_____

_____

notes

22
stick up for yourself

Comments and judgments from others make eating well more difficult. You may not be able to stop all comments, but if you let others know when their comments bother you, they will often stop. **What you eat, and how much, is up to you.**

Ideally, no one would make comments about what other people eat or don't eat, but that's not reality! **Eating together should first be about connection, not about what or how much each person eats.** But since TV shows, commercials, strangers, coworkers, and even teachers often feel it's okay to comment on others' food choices, you will get comments on your eating. Practice in advance what you might say to feel more confident when it comes up. You might rehearse in front of a mirror or role-play with your support person. Setting boundaries may include asking others who call you picky or comment on your eating to stop.

The following are some sample scripts for setting boundaries or deflecting comments from restaurant or cafeteria staff or fellow diners:

- "No thank you."
- "I'm all set here, thank you."
- "That's none of your business."
- "I'll think about what goes on my plate…"

- "Can we just order dessert please?"
- "I'm just not very hungry."
- You might ask your support partner to step in for you with, "We're doing fine here," Or, "Can you bring us the check?"

Find what works for you. You might want to explain or just be firm that you aren't discussing your eating.

Setting boundaries with family is hard for everyone. Even if you are no longer living at home and have your own home or job, your parents and others may still try to influence your eating. The following are some additional ideas for responding to comments during family meals. Adapt them or find your own words if you like:

- "I'm really enjoying dinner, but can we talk less about what or how much I'm eating?"
- "I know you are trying to help, and I appreciate it, but I'm learning the more other people pay attention to what or how much I'm eating, the less I feel like eating."
- "Let's talk about something else."
- "It upsets me when you make comments about my eating."
- You don't even have to say anything; you could even just walk away or leave the table.

notes

23
tune in to hunger and appetite

Many picky eaters are not able to tune in very well to hunger signals at first. There may be many reasons; perhaps those cues are subtler or harder to read (remember how some people can skip meals, while others feel very anxious or get headaches). Anxiety and stress dampen appetite, and study after study has shown that when people are pushed or coerced to do something (in this case eat), their resistance increases. Maybe you were told to finish your plate, or perhaps you were allowed to graze all day, so you never really had an *opportunity* to feel those signals—possibly since you were an infant!

We believe those signals can be buried because of all the challenges we have explored, but for the vast majority of people they do not *go away*. We believe you can learn to tune in to those cues and learn ways to reduce factors in your life that sabotage your hunger and appetite. (Remember that hunger refers more to the physical need for food, while appetite also includes the desire and anticipation of eating.) You've already learned some tips for dealing with anxiety, which impacts appetite. Now, let's explore supporting appetite.

Consider what hunger and appetite feel like for you. How does *your* body signal hunger? People experience hunger differently. There tend to be early hunger signals, and later signals that are generally less pleasant and can negatively impact your mood.

◆

The following list includes common feelings experienced by people when they need fuel. **Circle** any you have felt before:

headache

lightheaded feeling

vague anxiety

feeling shaky

stomach growling

difficulty concentrating

irritability

fatigue

nausea

vague discomfort or empty feeling in stomach or gut area

other _____

On the following outline of a body, mark an X where you think you might feel hunger and, using the preceding list, label the sensations. Use colored pencils or markers to draw your feelings if you have trouble naming them. What color does hungry feel like? Are the pencil strokes soft or bold?

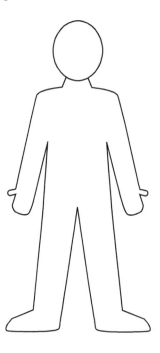

Some people report if they get very hungry or wait too long between eating opportunities (EOs), their hungry, gut-gnawing sensation can even go away. Have you experienced this? _____

Over the next few days, pay attention to your hunger signals to see if you think this might be happening to you. If it is, then creating a routine and planning ahead will be extra important.

describe and rate the intensity of your hunger

See if you can figure out which sensations on the previous page go along with each stage of hunger for you. Tune in at various times over the next few days and ask yourself:

Is it *early* hunger? Am I *a little* hungry?

_____

Am I *very* hungry? *Uncomfortably* hungry? _____

Am I still full from my last meal? What does that feel like?

_____

You might even use a scale as a quick way to gauge your hunger during the day.

 0—feel full, bloated, ate too much

1—still comfortably full from a previous EO

2—no signals or sensations of hunger

3—mild early signs of hunger

4—clear signs of hunger

5—uncomfortable and later signs of hunger

6—physical signs may be more intense or gone entirely

Thinking of appetite and hunger on this kind of continuum can help.

Now we will complicate things even more by throwing in the idea of "satisfaction," which is different than merely not being hungry. You may have had plenty of food, but not feel satisfied; for example, a meal does not seem complete until you enjoy one last bite, have a little something sweet, or sit and talk for a few minutes. See if you can begin to tell the difference between not feeling hungry an hour after a meal and feeling comfortably full right after a large meal. If you feel *uncomfortably* full, journal the physical sensations. Do you feel bloated, like it's hard to take a deep breath or you want to lie down? These different sensations will take time to tease apart once you start paying attention—something that many nonselective eaters struggle with as well.

eating well is flexible

When hunger signals are hard to hear: You may have heard the advice, "Eat when you're hungry, stop when you're full," but what if you can't reliably tell the difference yet? If you aren't sure what hungry feels like, you may learn best to identify hunger by satisfying it. If you eat and the feelings get better or go away, you were probably hungry. In the beginning, your hunger signals may seem like whispers. If you wait until you're hungry before you begin to rustle around in the fridge, you may get really hungry in the process and rely on a short list of familiar foods, or you may get beyond hungry and lose interest. Eating at regular intervals can help you discover and support appetite and hunger cues (explored in Chapter 25).

Eating when not hungry can nourish you: If low weight concerns are an issue, you will probably need to eat without hunger until those signals are more reliable. If this is the case, you should be working with a professional to establish a nourishing eating schedule.

If hunger makes you anxious, eating to avoid getting too hungry is kind to your body and spirit. Let's say you have a long meeting at work, a lecture, or a basketball game that occurs over your regular lunch or dinner time, and you know you'll become uncomfortably hungry. Some people eat a small amount to get their blood sugar up in preparation for a skipped meal and then offer themselves more to eat afterward.

Keep track of when you are hungriest for three days (you can use the food journal in Appendix II). Around what times do you generally eat?

_____

_____

_____

What are you usually doing before and while you eat?

_____

_____

When do you feel signs of hunger? First thing when you wake up? Right after school or work?

_____

_____

Advanced: **See how different foods impact hunger.** If you only drink juice or soda and eat a few crackers, you've consumed quick energy that doesn't stick around for long and you may feel hungry fairly soon after eating. You may notice if you eat foods containing fats, protein, or fiber (French fries or peanut butter on whole wheat, for example), you may feel more satisfied and not feel hungry for a few hours. For example, if I (Katja) have a bowl of cereal flakes and milk for breakfast, I'm quite hungry within an hour and a half. If I eat whole-wheat toast with peanut butter and jam, half a banana, and a glass of milk, I'm not hungry for about three hours.

Check in a few times *after* meals in the next few days.

What did you eat? _____

Did you eat a small, average, or large amount for you? _____

What did you feel physically? _____

How long until you felt your first signs of hunger? _____

Many selective eaters, particularly if they were thought to be too small or not eating enough as children, were encouraged to eat or drink throughout the day (grazing), up to many times an hour. This can take away early hunger cues and make it harder to eat to fullness. It's why almost all pediatric feeding therapists recommend having time between eating—to allow the opportunity for hunger to develop. It may seem counterintuitive, but not grazing tends to lead to eating greater amounts. Taking the "edge" off hunger is not the same thing as eating to fullness. Eating to fullness may take some getting used to if you've been nibbling or sipping throughout the day for years.

To be clear, in no way are we suggesting you "get" yourself to eat to the point of discomfort. Some people have been pushed to eat large amounts of food in an effort to make them gain weight rapidly. This generally means eating beyond comfortably full. While eating based on your own hunger and fullness signals may be unfamiliar territory, you are working toward building trust with your body and tuning in to what *you* know to be true about yourself when you eat.

A repeat reminder: if you are struggling to gain needed weight, this should be done under the supervision of a medical and therapy team.

notes

24
be present in your body while you eat

It is natural to want to distract yourself from a task that is unpleasant but unavoidable. Using distraction to get nutrients in can be a matter of survival, or at the very least, a means of minimizing unpleasant feelings or attention from others. In fact, some feeding therapies encourage children to deliberately tune out hunger and fullness cues. These therapies get food and drinks into the child through rewards such as toys or screen time—which can override signals from the child's body. Parents have described this to us as the child being "zoned out" while eating.

In urgent situations, it may make sense to distract to get energy in; for example, if you are losing weight or unable to maintain weight, professional help is important, and using distraction tools may be part of an early treatment plan. However, relying on these techniques over time can slow progress with eating. It becomes difficult to transition from tuned-out to *tuned-in* eating, a skill that takes time to learn or relearn.

If your weight is stable and you've learned to only feel comfortable eating with a distraction such as a screen or book, this strategy that once served your needs may now get in the way of learning more about your hunger and appetite cues.

◆

How do you use distractions? Circle any activity you do regularly while eating:

texting or talking on the phone   standing up at the counter or walking around

watching a screen   working at desk or on laptop

reading   driving or riding in a car or bus

playing games   other _____

How much you rely on distractions can provide some clues and goals to work toward. We envision this as a continuum. Where do you fall now? After the following statements, indicate:

Strongly Agree, Agree, Disagree, Strongly Disagree:

I don't eat unless I have a screen or book _____

I can eat without distraction, but I much prefer to eat with it _____

Sometimes I watch TV or read if I'm eating alone, but I'm happy and not anxious when eating without distraction _____

I eat less, or can't eat, if there *is* a distraction _____

◆

Being in your body. Sit on a chair with your feet flat on the floor; perhaps even take off your shoes first. Push against the floor, feeling the chair or bench under your bottom. Feel held up by the ground and the seat. Put your hands on your knees, palms down, and take three deep breaths. This can help you feel more "grounded" and centered and less scattered. Close your eyes if you want to.

Weaning off distractions. If the idea of getting rid of your screen or book for most meals makes you uncomfortable or causes you to think you will eat less, consider weaning slowly from a screen rather than quitting all at once. The following are some options to try over the coming days:

- Use a screen for only the first or last five minutes of a meal or snack.

- Pick one meal or snack to eat without a screen. See how that goes. If it goes well, add another meal or snack.

- Turn off distractions for three minutes at any time during a meal or snack. How did that feel?

    _____

    Then try it again, maybe for four minutes this time. Give yourself permission to turn the screen on at any time, but see if you can make it.

- Try not to use the screen when eating with others. If they know not to comment on what or how much you eat, you might not need a screen to protect you from comments.

What helped you wean from a screen or distractions?

_____

_____

Where are you feeling stuck?

_____

_____

Being present can deepen your ability to tune in to your body, but tuning out a little can help get you over a hurdle. Sometimes a little distraction, such as eating with chopsticks or your nondominant hand (put the fork in your left hand if you usually eat with your right), can make a new food feel more accessible. Perhaps use a toothpick to eat noodles or veggies from a bowl of soup.

Eating in an unfamiliar way can decrease anxiety and help you "forget" why you think you won't like a food. **For more challenging foods, you can strategically use distraction** such as a favorite comedy or YouTube clip.

◆

Here's something to ponder. If you use a screen, do you want to get rid of it? Let's face it, eating alone can be boring. If you can eat without a screen and don't think it's a problem, you can continue to watch the screen. If you don't feel ready to work on distractions yet, consider working on the next exercise on eating at regular intervals, and then come back to this issue of distractions. Wait until you have a good routine of eating every two to four hours with your distractions.

notes

25
support appetite with regular meals and snacks

Now that you've explored hunger cues a little, you can move on to the next step—establishing a routine around eating. This can be a tough habit to get into, so it's a long chapter. You'll begin to work through it over the next few days to weeks, but it can take months for a routine to become second nature. People often find they feel better with regular meals and snacks and don't feel well when that daily rhythm falls apart.

Routine supports eating because for most people, the body has natural rhythms around food. You eat, saliva (spit) begins to break down food, the stomach breaks down food further, and nutrients begin to be absorbed into the body as the hormone (chemical messenger) insulin is released to deal with the energy in the form of broken-down sugars in your bloodstream. There's much more to it, but our blood sugar level is a big actor controlling hunger and energy.

If you worry you weigh too much or are gaining weight, skipping meals and chaotic eating is likely to make things worse, meaning weight gain may continue rapidly. In teens, dieting is a predictor of weight gain, disordered eating behaviors, and depression. However, some selective eaters are larger than average *and* healthy.

The exercises and strategies in this book equally apply whether you are smaller or bigger than average. Attuned or intuitive eating that responds to internal cues of hunger and fullness supports good health. Research by Ellyn Satter, a renowned childhood feeding expert, on "eating competent" adults shows these adults plan to eat (and tend to get better nutrition) rather than follow chaotic eating patterns. Adults who eat regularly and are eating competent tend to have more stable weight and enjoy better health. If you are worried you weigh too much or are gaining weight rapidly, eating at regular times and nourishing yourself with food is far more likely to lead to healthier and more stable weight than dieting.

Consider seeing your doctor to rule out medical causes of weight gain if you are concerned. Review Chapter 13 for ways to support your health now. See Appendix III for more information on weight and health.

You might be tired of these reminders, but if it has been determined that you are losing weight or measure below your expected weight, you need to work with trained professionals to improve your eating competence and nutritional status.

Getting into a routine supports appetite and makes internal cues easier to discover and tune into.

Track your schedule for three days. (You can use the space in the following pages or make copies of the Food Journal in Appendix II or print them out from the PDF on our website: www.extremepickyeatinghelp.com/ teenadultresources). Where are you starting from? Write down when, what, and where you are eating and when you get up, go to bed, and go to school or work. In the notes section, describe if anyone in your household cooked, whether you were eating with others, and how you were feeling. Track this on your phone if you prefer. You can even take pictures of the foods and surroundings to jog your memory.

	Time	Food	Notes
Day 1			
Day 2			
Day 3			

Now see if you can make some changes. You may try to change everything at once, but most people feel less overwhelmed if they pick one change to start and add another change every week or so.

Try the following ideas for changing your routine:

Within 30 minutes of getting out of bed in the morning, sit down to eat—or eat on-the-go if that works. Make a change for three days. How did that go?

_____

_____

Sit down to eat every two to four hours for three days. Set an alarm on your phone or watch if you need to remind yourself. You don't have to eat much, or at all, but sit down with food in front of you. Apps like Aloe Bud can help you remember to take care of yourself in areas such as sleep, eating, and medications.

How did it go?

_____

_____

review

How easy or hard was it to make the time to change your routine? _____

Which was easier: weekends or weekdays? _____

What got in the way of establishing an eating routine? Check all that apply.

_____ work responsibilities   _____ school

_____ extra projects   _____ doctor or therapy

_____ social outings   _____ appointments

_____ sports/working out   _____ not enough money to buy food

_____ commute   _____ didn't like what was available

other _____

Let's look at an example of an 18 year-old high school student without a lot of eating structure and see where he could start making some changes. The following describes Jacob's typical day of eating:

7 am: Alarm goes off to get ready for school. He does not feel hungry and is rushed, so he goes to school without eating.

7:45 am: Arrives at school. He feels sluggish and finds it hard to concentrate.

10 am: He gets a Coke and Cheez-Its from a vending machine between classes.

Noon: Lunch break. Heads to drive-through for fries, a plain hamburger and a Coke.

2-5 pm: Heads to work. Asked to join friend from work for dinner but doesn't because he doesn't like Chinese food.

6 pm: Returns home and plays video games to unwind.

8 pm: After his parents have dinner, Jacob realizes he's very hungry and eats three slices of leftover plain cheese pizza and some microwave popcorn.

9-11 pm: Does homework then watches TV and texts with friends until tired.

Midnight: Jacob usually goes to sleep.

Brainstorm how Jacob might be able to make some kind of breakfast happen. (Hint: Start with foods he already eats.)

_____

_____

To kick-start his routine, perhaps Jacob could have a granola bar, a bag of microwave popcorn, a glass of milk and a granola bar, or a bag of dry cereal as he is getting ready or even in the car on the way to school.

> Remember, when you are beginning to establish your routine, eat what you eat now. Don't worry about what you eat, just *when*. Plan meals and snacks, or eating opportunities (EOs), every three to four hours (ideally no more frequently than every two hours). Drink water in between.

If his first EO is close to 7:30 am, having a snack at 10:30 is reasonable. He could continue to buy food from the vending machine or pack something from home. He may need to buy an insulated lunch bag with a cool pack or a small cooler to keep food in his locker or car. For lunch around noon, Jacob could pack some cold pizza or continue to stop at a drive-through. Remember, for now, he is concentrating on eating every two to four hours, not necessarily on changing his food choices—unless he wants to.

You may have noticed his lunch hour is scheduled only an hour and a half after his snack break. While it isn't ideal to eat more frequently than every two hours, for Jacob it's better than waiting five hours, from 7:00 a.m. until noon. This is because **in general, it's best to have an EO sooner rather than wait too long, which can lead to anxiety or feeling uncomfortably hungry. Jacob does the best he can with school and work demands and you will too. Your routine should allow for some wiggle room throughout the day.**

"I wouldn't eat at school, and then I'd be starving when I got home. I'd inhale two bagels with melted cheese. When I started bringing food for lunch, I could stop and think about what I wanted to eat after school. I still eat lots of bagels with cheese, but I've added a few more options. I've even started making smoothies with vanilla yogurt and frozen bananas."
—Kenzie, 15-year-old high school student

◆

Establishing a routine doesn't mean you can't ever eat between meals and snacks. It means that most days, you aim to not wait too long between meals or nibble all day. Sometimes, if a meal was rushed or you were distracted by getting back to work or doing something fun, you may have ended a meal before you had enough. If you ever feel hungry and think you can't—or don't want to—wait until the next planned meal or snack, honor that hunger and nourish yourself!

Thinking ahead about food for times when you will be away from home can be a difficult habit to get into. If you are out and about, think about a portable food that might fill you up. Some ideas include:

- granola or energy bar
- bag of potato chips
- yogurt drink and crackers
- fast-food fries
- packet of cashews or nuts that you like
- plain bagel and cream cheese
- baggie of dry cereal and an apple

Write down three portable options of foods that you eat:

1. _____

2. _____

3. _____

Think about where you want to eat and with whom. You might count on a take-out at lunch or choose to join in with family members at their meals.

Write down the names of some people with whom you might eat.

_____

_____

_____

Write down some options for lunch foods away from home.

_____

_____

_____

_____

◆

Planning for and eating around the same times every day is a process. You may do well for several days, and then have a weekend of chaos. That's okay. You may feel like eating with your parents or friends, or feel like exploring things by yourself for a time. Consider Jacob. While he was getting into a routine, he didn't feel ready to eat with his parents. They had a long history of arguing at dinner time, and he wanted to work on his eating first. He hasn't eaten with his parents since early high school. He does think he might be ready to join them for weekly pizza dinners soon, though. He's also begun to share some of his progress with them.

26
make a three-meal menu plan

Hopefully you are making some progress with eating about every three or four (not more frequently than every two) hours. If not, spend a little more time with the last chapter before moving on. Once routine is, well, more routine for you, consider adding more food variety. **Start with a mealtime you already eat regularly, such as weekend breakfasts or lunches, and include familiar foods. Add more variety from there**.

Before you continue, if you haven't looked at your list of food preferences in Appendix I in a while, do so now. Have any of the foods changed categories, say from "interested to try" to "eat now and enjoy?" Have any foods moved up from "can't imagine trying?" If so, take a moment to recognize your progress. Updating your list as you begin to enjoy more foods will help with menu planning. Don't forget that progress isn't just about the list. If you feel more confident and less anxious overall, even if your list remains unchanged, that's moving in the right direction.

◆

Write down the foods for three meals that include one of the foods you regularly eat as well as something you can stretch toward: a food you sometimes eat or have eaten in the past.

1. _____

2. _____

3. _____

For three days, write down roughly when you will try to eat, using the tables on the following page. Have access to one or two accepted foods with every meal or snack. Include the three meals you wrote down above and try to fill the rest in from your preferences list. You can leave blanks for now if it feels overwhelming or plan one day ahead. Read below for ideas based on our friend Jacob from Chapter 25. You can also use the Food Journal in Appendix II.

DAY 1

TIME	FOODS

DAY 2

TIME	FOODS

DAY 3

TIME	FOODS

Don't forget to have your preferred condiments or sauces available!

The following shows how Jacob might build three days of meals and snacks, starting with his food preferences list:

Favored foods: round Tostitos tortilla chips, pretzels, lightly buttered pasta (preferably elbow macaroni), white rice, plain Lenders bagel, Wendy's plain hamburger, popcorn, McDonald's chicken nuggets (no sauce), plain cheese pizza (no crusts), cheese quesadilla, fries, vanilla ice cream

Accepted foods: vanilla yogurt, grilled cheese on white, green grapes, peeled apples, bananas, microwaved frozen corn with small amount of butter, Goldfish crackers, 2% strawberry milk, granola bars with chocolate chips

Not eating yet: other fresh fruit or vegetables, mixed textures

Characteristics of preferred foods: crunchy and salty, but smooth and salty work too

Condiments: ketchup, ranch dressing, butter, salt

sample menu, eat every three to four hours

Breakfast: Lender's bagel, half a cut-up banana, vanilla yogurt (not fat-free to include some fat)

Morning and/or afternoon snack (depending on timing): pretzels, green grapes, 2% strawberry milk

Lunch: cut-up apple with half the slices peeled (experimenting with leaving apple skin on while still having peeled apples as an option), cinnamon-sugar (which he used to enjoy as a young child) shaker on the table, chicken nuggets, pretzels

Dinner: plain rice, some chicken breast leftover from his parents' earlier dinner, green grapes, ketchup on the table, vanilla ice cream for dessert

Jacob's sample menu demonstrates that each meal and snack features accepted foods with a few more challenging choices showing up here and there (see how to stretch to new foods in Chapters 31 and 33). When building a meal or snack, there are two equally acceptable approaches you can choose from. One way is to think of foods in terms of four basic "food groups," which include grains/starch, dairy, fruits and veggies, and meat/meat substitute. Or you can use the "macro" (main) nutrient building blocks of carbohydrate/starch, fat, protein, and fiber (generally in fruits and veggies). If you don't or can't eat dairy, thinking in terms of macronutrients may make it easier to cover your nutrition bases. Go with whichever approach you are most comfortable with. For a bit more on menu planning, see Appendix IV.

Don't worry about portion sizes. Let your body and preferences tell you how much of the foods you want to eat. Even if Jacob doesn't eat any apple slices, putting a few on the table is important. He might eat 10 chicken nuggets and then feel like eating lots of grapes for a snack. As you learned in Chapter 17, it's okay to not eat everything you put out, and you can get more pretzels or apple slices if you want them.

Writing the menu helps you imagine options, whether or not you stick to it closely. This is a skill that takes time to develop. You might plan a menu—but be prepared for life to happen! Making changes, relying on accepted foods, or eating out are all options, and giving yourself permission to be imperfect increases your odds of success.

How did it feel to write a three-meal menu plan?

_____

_____

Was your preferences list helpful to the process?

_____

Did you plan meals in terms of food groups or macronutrients? (Check out Appendix IV if this was hard.)

_____

What did you find challenging in terms of writing the menu?

_____

If you ate meals from the menu plan, did you stick closely to the plan or make changes? If you made changes, how did that work out?

_____

_____

_____

Advanced: **See if you can find some of those recipes that looked good from earlier exercises.** When you control how food is prepared, you have the power to change a recipe! If a recipe calls for fresh cilantro and you aren't sure if you like it or don't want to include it, you can leave it out or serve it on the side. If you don't love cooked onions, skip them for now!

27
recognize early progress

Progress may feel slow, and you almost certainly won't be trying sushi overnight. It may also feel as though you make a step forward, only to take two steps back by reaching for familiar foods on a tough day. **It is important not to miss early signs of progress.** Knowing what to look for, and seeing early progress as an essential part of the journey, will help you reach your goals.

Think about this scenario: your goal is to run a 5K race, but hypothetically you don't yet know how to crawl. If you thought progress only meant running, you would get discouraged and quit. However, if you recognized that pulling yourself up on your hands and knees, then crawling, and then walking had to happen before you could run, then crawling would feel pretty exciting! Progress!

Many selective eaters experience a typical pattern of progress. In the early stages, there may be less anxiety or noticing hints of hunger. Then anxiety continues to decrease, along with a budding curiosity about foods: a recipe that "doesn't look so bad," an increased comfort with new foods being closer on the table, or touching/prepping a new food without issue.

It may take weeks or months of focusing on the steps of eating regularly and offering yourself the opportunity to explore new foods before you feel ready to try them. Some foods may be easier to try sooner, like a new flavor of ice cream. You might see some early signs of progress and go back and forth between the fluid "stages" of progress.

> Rubi shared this observation of her progress: "*After seeing carrots on the table many times, even helping to peel, chop, and cook them, I finally tasted a raw carrot with ranch dressing and was surprised it wasn't awful.*"

Check all of the early signs of progress that apply to you:

_____ able to sit at a table and tolerate challenging foods at the table

_____ able to go to a restaurant and feel less anxious

_____ spending less time thinking or worrying about food

_____ planning for occasional meals and snacks in advance

_____ beginning to sense hunger or fullness cues

_____ tolerating or being curious about new foods

_____ other _____

Check all of the later signs of progress that apply to you:

____ touching or tasting a new food

____ being curious

____ thinking a new recipe looks good

____ cooking or fixing food more often

____ eating meals with people who used to impact my appetite negatively

What other signs of progress have you noticed? How do you feel things have improved?

_____

_____

_____

_____

> For some, enjoying food may be a late step of progress. You may find progress in the absence of overwhelmingly negative feelings or a particular food's upgrade from "disgusting" to "tolerable." Everyone has a distinct history, process, and trajectory of progress, even if there are some similarities.

check in

How are you doing with distractions? Review Chapter 24 on screens and distractions. Did you slip back into using a screen with most meals and snacks, or have you been using it less and haven't even noticed?

_____

_____

_____

What impacts your screen or book use? (If your answer includes stress, review Chapter 20.)

_____

_____

28
plan for success while eating out

Eating out can be especially challenging, with unfamiliar food, decor, staff, and worry that a waiter or fellow diner might joke about your menu choice. **You may decide to eat out less or get take-out in the beginning. That's a great choice if it feels right. It's okay to pick your challenges.** Pick the areas where you want to focus your energies, such as eating regularly or accepting what foods you do eat. On the other hand, you might enjoy eating out and feel ready for a new challenge! How you feel about it might change from one week to the next. Being in touch with the "how" and "why" of your feelings will help you know when, and in what ways, you are ready to investigate new experiences.

◆

Control what you can. Try these ideas when you eat out. See what works for you.

- Suggest a familiar restaurant.
- If it is a new place: browse the menu online and look for familiar foods, and/or eat something light at home before you go out. When at new places, try to eat with people who support you.
- Focus on enjoying the outing with friends and family. Say something like, "Hey, while food isn't something I get too excited about, I really look forward to just hanging out with you."

  As one client shared, "At new restaurants, I look at the menu online for a few things I think I can eat, then focus on having fun with my friends. Sometimes I eat a small snack beforehand so I'm not starving. Being really hungry makes me anxious because I'm never sure if there will be food I can actually eat."

Restaurants that have a buffet are a great place to start. You can take small amounts of different items (reduces worry about waste), and the cost is generally less than dinner entrées. Certain buffets, including Chinese or Indian restaurants, have options that many people can eat, including rice and naan (a flat white bread).

Try a restaurant with a buffet and write down your observations.

_____

_____

_____

If you were able to enjoy just bread or dessert without feeling embarrassed you weren't eating anything else, noticed positive changes in your feelings about eating out, or enjoyed part or all of the experience, these are all signs of early progress we reviewed in the last exercise.

notes

_____

_____

_____

_____

_____

_____

_____

_____

_____

_____

_____

_____

_____

_____

_____

_____

_____

_____

29
change the environment

A change in your surroundings, like heading to college, a summer camp, staying with a friend or relative, moving to a new town, or traveling abroad can be a time of awakening and discovery. Several adults have shared that a trip overseas was the first time they branched out to new foods; the food can be totally different, there are few expectations, and you are out of your usual comfort zone. They talked about permission from host families to approach foods with caution; not having many options; being away from home and all the reminders of how they usually ate; embracing the trip as a mind-shifting opportunity to try new things; finding acceptable foods to explore such as rice, pasta, or flatbreads; and the way foods were served.

> *"I did an internship in Japan. I loved the restaurants where you could grill at the table on skewers, there were ramen places where I could pick out what I didn't want to eat, and there was even Japanese fried chicken. I felt like I had control. I think the fact that everything was new helped. No one there pressured me to eat things. I think they expected me to be picky since I was American. I was totally polite and was treated well. I also went in with this attitude of openness. I still don't eat raw fish, but I found enough to eat to survive, and I have continued to add more foods back at home."*
> —26-year-old working in public relations

In China, many restaurants serve foods on a "lazy Susan," a circular, spinning tray of food placed on the middle of the table. No more passing bowls; instead, you just gently spin the lazy Susan until you can reach what you want, and watch others serving themselves and trying the food.

You might not be able to travel or live abroad, but you can try adapting some international approaches. Try a restaurant with totally unfamiliar food, travel to a large U.S. city and try some food trucks, get a lazy Susan and eat family style the Chinese way, watch some cooking shows with a new cuisine, and try a different ethnic recipe.

When traveling, it's okay to take along some familiar foods so you know you won't go hungry. When we (Katja and family) travel, we often take trail mix, mixed nuts, or granola bars. When my daughter was little, we brought a jar of Miracle Whip with us to visit family in France. We got teased about it, of course, but it was her favorite condiment at the time.

Do a little advance research on your destination. What are the typical breakfasts like? In Germany, for example, breakfast may include boiled eggs, sliced cheese, what we think of as "lunch meats," crusty white rolls with butter, and granola. Some meals may go better than others. See if you can find a hotel with a buffet.

Even in new situations, stick with your eating routine when you can. If you are walking around a town, have your snacks with you and enjoy a crusty loaf of white bread or a scoop or two of ice cream in a city square. Think of how you can get enough fuel. Rely on your accepted foods if you need to.

> *"I mostly ate tortillas, rice and cereal at home. When I went to college there were so many options. The meal plan meant I could pick and choose at the cafeteria. Something clicked for me, and I felt like I could try new things. When I went back home though I still wanted cereal. My parents didn't believe me when I told them what I was eating at school. I'm working on figuring out how I can change things at home too."*
> — Angel, age 19

Is there a time when you were in a new place or with new people where you felt curious about new foods, or were able to reach beyond your comfort zone? If yes, can you consider why? What was it that helped you feel more open, and can you imagine bringing that curiosity into your everyday life now?

_____

_____

_____

_____

_____

_____

_____

30
it's your plate and your body

When people don't feel in control, they also feel they aren't the ones deciding what happens to their bodies (autonomy), including what they eat or drink. This can lead to anxiety. Your plate is your space. Insist whenever possible that you plate (serve) your own food. Whether plating takes place at the stove or, ideally, at the table with serving plates and bowls, you control what, how much, and where food goes on your plate. For more control of your plate, consider using plates fashioned after compartmentalized cafeteria trays. You may feel more comfortable having a saucy food on your plate if you know the sauce won't run into another food. You can find plates like these at many department stores or online, and they go right into the dishwasher.

> **Here's an empathy thought experiment for family and friends.** Ask friends and family members to name a food they *hate*, something they find disgusting, or something that made them sick or nauseated and took them a long time to feel comfortable eating again. For many people, something will come to mind quickly, which can help them empathize with you. Then ask, or write down, these thought questions for them: "What if every time you sat down to eat, a small amount of _____ (fill in their disliked food) was on your plate? Even if you didn't have to eat it, how would it feel to sit down to that plate? What if you had to smell it and look at it, even if you liked the other foods on your plate? What if, at every meal, you were expected to take one bite or even lick that food before you were allowed to eat the foods you liked? Might you get annoyed or feel put out, controlled, or resentful? Would your appetite be impacted? Might you leave the table without eating and try to get food later, or even sneak into the kitchen?"
>
> Most will answer they wouldn't like it and even become upset, that they would not enjoy meals as much. This is another way to help people who enjoy a variety of foods to empathize with you.

Have a paper napkin available when you eat so you can spit out food. You will likely be more willing to try a new food if you know you can spit it out. (You can do this discreetly.) Note: If you spit food out more than a few times a day, or if you spit food out because you don't want the calories or you can't swallow, these are serious signs of more disordered eating that indicate a need for professional help.

Buffets are another way to take control of what goes on your plate, as are restaurant chains that serve foods "family style " (in large serving bowls at the table).

notes

31

mindful eating activities
to help you explore and discover

Learning to enjoy a variety of foods is a *process* of discovery. This chapter is about paying attention and discovering what you like and why, and how you might approach new foods.

> Lara, 24, ate mostly versions of bread and cheese. One of her goals was to learn to enjoy apples. During mindful eating exercises, she tried small bites of apple, then bigger bites. She then tried apples with the skin on, cut thin, then thicker without the peel. Lara had an "aha" moment when she took a larger bite of apple and realized she felt less tense and anxious than with smaller bites. The tiny pieces she had always been told to try seemed to get lost in her mouth, and she discovered she felt anxious when they made it to the back of her throat, and she sometimes gagged. Bigger bites felt more manageable. Lara was excited to learn that larger bites of peeled apples felt safer, and she enjoyed the flavor, even as she was getting used to the crunch and juices.

With mindful eating activities, the goal is to pay attention, learning what you enjoy and building on those discoveries at your own pace. You might figure out that, like Lara, larger bites feel less scary than smaller bites, or you might learn the opposite. There are no right or wrong reactions to a mindful eating experiment.

Every experience with food is an opportunity to collect data and be curious about your reactions. When Lara gagged on small bites, she didn't beat herself up and assume she "failed;" instead, she learned that smaller bites triggered her gagging. Each attempt with a new food may result in different outcomes. Mindful eating experiences also help decrease anxiety and offer "exposures" to new things in a safe environment.

> **About the term "exposure:"** Some therapies use "escape extinction" or other "exposure" therapies called "flooding," in which someone is exposed to a scary stimulus (anything someone is afraid of, such as a food or spiders) in a way that can feel very overwhelming. The idea is to repeatedly expose the subject to the upsetting stimulus in order to neutralize the fear. In many cases, we have seen this kind of therapy *worsen* anxiety and selective eating, with clients vomiting and panicking in the parking lot before therapy sessions—sometimes for weeks.
>
> For the purposes of this book, and in our work, "exposure" means something

different: an opportunity to safely interact with a new food through your senses, including sight, smell, touch, and taste. A first-step exposure may include looking at a cookbook or seeing a certain food across the table. Each exposure you choose is an opportunity to learn about the food, to pay attention to your reactions and to practice skills managing those reactions, including anxiety. In addition, repeated exposures to foods this way often lead to acceptance and enjoyment of these foods over time.

Note: If you are dealing with low appetite and any worries about poor weight gain, the initial focus of meals and snack times should be on eating enough of familiar foods and feeling comfortable. For many, as long as there is an accepted food on the table and no coercion to try new foods, meals provide a natural place for a blossoming curiosity about new foods. Passing potatoes or smelling the meatballs may lead to putting some on your plate and, eventually, taking a taste. For others, trying new foods is challenging to the point that it can bring up stress and decrease appetite; in this case, it may be best to try new foods and mindful eating activities *separate* from meal and snack times.

mindful eating activities checklist

Consider having the following items on hand as you explore new foods:

- paper napkin (for spitting out food if you need to)

- favorite condiments

- accepted food (foods you can dip are ideal for trying new soups or sauces)

- favorite drink (can help to clear a taste if you don't enjoy it)

- supportive people (or alone)—see what works for you

  "Mindful" eating is about curiosity. As you experience different ways of exploring the food, before you try it, say out loud: **"I wonder what will happen if I take tiny bites?"** Then, **"I wonder what will happen if I take bigger bites?"**

mindful eating activities

Set aside 15 minutes and take some deep breaths before you start. Stop when you feel you are done, which at first might be after only a few bites or a few moments. You may want to start doing this activity twice a week; however, as often or as infrequently as you are comfortable with is the right amount.

Start with a food you eat regularly. What did you choose? _____

Before you take a bite, what does it look like? _____

Close your eyes and take a moment to smell the food. If it has a strong odor, try just waving a bit of the aroma under your nose instead of inhaling deeply. What do you notice?

_____

different ways to explore foods

_____ taking very small bites

_____ chewing with your molars

_____ chewing with only your front teeth

_____ taking bigger bites

_____ exploring the food with your tongue

_____ placing the food in the middle of your tongue before you chew and swallow

_____ placing the food directly between your molars and chewing, then swallowing

Pick at least two ways to explore the accepted food you chose for your first mindful eating experiment. What did you pick?

_____

Did you learn anything about your familiar food? Did you prefer one way of exploring the food over another, such as smaller or larger bites? Did the way you chewed impact the experience?

_____

_____

_____

If you felt like you might gag, can you identify when? Before you put the food in your mouth? When you chewed? When you tried to swallow?

_____

_____

For each session, explore a food in one or more different ways. A few bites with attention might take three to five minutes.

◆

Now that you are familiar with the process and have some observations on an accepted food, you may be ready to challenge yourself a bit. Refer to your food preferences list you were asked to fill out in the back of the book, in Appendix I. If you haven't yet filled in this list, take some time and do so now. From the list, choose five foods from the second category of "eat now but don't enjoy" and write them down below.

1. _____

2. _____

3. _____

4. _____

5. _____

Pick two of the five foods that feel least challenging or intrigue you. Then choose at least two ways to explore the foods from the list.

Which foods did you pick and why?

1. _____

2. _____

Which ways did you decide to explore?

_____

_____

What did you observe?

_____

_____

_____

Wait a few days and try the same foods again. Look back at the different ways to explore the food with attention and try something new. Was it easier the second or third time? Are you continuing to discover new things about the foods? Write down some of your observations.

_____

_____

_____

_____

If you discovered you prefer big bites of an accepted food, is that true for a more challenging food?

_____

◆

If you discovered one of the foods interested you, was enjoyable, or was at least not unpleasant, plan to put a small amount of this food in a small bowl or on a plate along with your accepted foods at mealtime.

Describe what that was like. For example, did you focus on it? Did you want to try it or put it on your plate? Did it impact your appetite or enjoyment of the meal in positive or negative ways?

_____

_____

◆

If you found you didn't want to put the food out or it was distracting you from your enjoyment of the meal, let this part go. It may take months to want to introduce new foods at mealtimes.

Review the signs of anxiety on page 20. If you are feeling anxious or panicky while doing this activity drop back to a less challenging food or stop for a few days.

> If these eating explorations are routinely difficult or dreaded, sometimes the added attention to the process feels pressuring. You don't have to do mindful eating exercises at all. You may be a person who does better with less focused, more natural exposures in day-to-day meal settings or eating out. You may do better going with the flow or feel more curious some days over others. You may also decide eventually to take this step a few months down the road, or with a therapist who can guide you through relaxation and exploring new foods if you are stuck.
>   "I never did 'mindful' eating. For me it felt forced and brought up all the times I was made to eat things when I was little. Having a fiancée who likes to cook, and who knows what's up and what I need, has helped. In the last year, I've been finding new foods I like because they are on the table and I'm curious. Many times, though, my fiancée has cooked something and I just don't take any, and that's okay too. I think if I had to sit down and make it into, like, homework, I'd resent it."
>   — Grace, age 36

You've come to the end of a long and potentially challenging chapter. Read through the chapter and your notes again now to synthesize your discoveries.

notes

_____

_____

_____

_____

_____

_____

_____

_____

_____

_____

_____

_____

_____

_____

_____

_____

32
discover what *smells* good

Up to now, you may have been using your sense of sight, taste, and vision to interact with foods. Smell may be a way to identify foods that are promising and enjoyable, or at least not unpleasant. Research tells us a large part of how we experience taste comes from our sense of smell.

◆

Go to your kitchen and pull out some spice jars from the cupboard and sauces from the fridge. Start with one or two if this feels challenging, or start with 10 if you like. Write down the name of the spices and/or sauces. If any are interesting or pleasant, see if you can describe why.

_____

_____

_____

_____

Offer yourself any sauces or dips that smelled interesting or good. Put a small amount of the sauce in a bowl or saucer on the table during meals or snacks. That may be enough for the first few times or you may feel ready to dip an accepted food into the new sauce. You can lick the sauce off or take a bite. If you remembered to put out a paper napkin, you always have the option of discreetly spitting something out. When you discover you enjoy a new sauce or dip, add it to your accepted condiments list.

Search online for simple recipes that include the spices that smelled good to you, and pick one to make. Alternatively, sprinkle the spice onto an accepted food, such as plain cooked chicken breast, or mix a bit into a little corn muffin batter and bake a few flavored muffins. Use a colored toothpick to label the different flavors.

Some larger cities have spice retailers, such as Penzey's, or spice departments in higher-end grocery outlets. These are a great place to explore spices. They usually carry samples to smell and free recipe cards.

notes

33
build on what you like

Pathways to discovering new foods are often called fading, chaining, stretching, bridging, linking, or leaping. Essentially, these terms all mean taking a food you like and changing something about it in small ways or thinking of something new with a similar food preparation (for example fried chicken tenders if you like chicken nuggets). You can also try new foods with a familiar sauce or texture as the link or bridge. You probably already do this to a degree. If you can eat bread or tortillas, you probably try different brands or offerings from different restaurants. There are many ways to bridge to new foods: flavors, sauces and dips, temperature, textures you like, flavors in liquids and drinks, combining with other foods, or starting with sweets.

> I (Jenny) did not eat cheese as a child, although everyone in my family did. My negative feelings about cheese were further cemented during a traumatic experience: my friend decided to force a large chunk of cheddar cheese into my mouth, holding a hand over my mouth so I couldn't spit it out. Many years went by (with no cheese consumed), and I found myself at a gathering at a family friend's house where cheese was served along with other hors d'oeuvres (appetizers). A trusted friend offered some cheese, I declined, and she gently suggested that I try a tiny bit of Brie (explaining that it was very mild) on the corner of a cracker with a grape in the same bite. I discovered it was not bad, tried more on my own later, and now enjoy many varieties of cheese. I still like cheese with a cracker and a grape! This story demonstrates several opportunities that helped me branch out: the new cheese was linked with two foods I already liked, I had a supportive and nonjudgmental friend who was able to explain and prepare me for how it might taste, I knew I could fill up on crackers, and I started with just a little bit of cheese.

First, why do you like what you like/tolerate? Review the "foods I eat now" list in the food preferences table in the back of the book in Appendix I. What characteristics do these foods you eat now have in common? Use description words such as crunchy, sweet, salty.

_____

_____

_____

Once you identify what you like about foods you eat now, you can bridge to other foods with similar characteristics. If you like crunchy things, you might branch out with new flavors of potato chips you like, or try a veggie straw or freeze-dried snap peas. For example, if you like tortilla chips, you might bridge to a different shape of the same chip. You might dip it into a mild salsa (dip, not scoop at first), crumble the chips to sprinkle on top of a food, or add crunch to a sandwich. Can you write out some possible chains or bridges?

_____ to _____

_____ to _____

_____ to _____

_____ to _____

_____ to _____

bridge with sauces, dips, spreads, and sprinkles

Condiments are a great way to connect or stretch a preferred food to a newer food. For some time, you might want ketchup or hot sauce on many or most new foods you try. That's okay! Don't worry you will get "stuck" on condiments; we like to think of them as "training wheels," if that helps you. Research tells us that when children are learning to like vegetables, condiments such as ranch dressing or a small amount of brown sugar makes them taste better and feel familiar. Condiments can be a great tool to widen the number of foods you enjoy.

- **Have condiments/sprinkles available** at every meal and snack.

- **"Sprinkles"** may be your favorite cracker or pretzel crumbled into pieces.

- **Rethink the definition of condiment:** peanut butter, hummus, frosting, Nutella, yogurt. Dip or spread away!

- **Try new condiments.** Can you get a sauce packet at a restaurant? If you like salty flavors, you might like soy or teriyaki sauce. If you enjoy spicy, you might try Sriracha, spicy mustard, wasabi, or hot sauce. You could "fade" a new flavor into an accepted sauce, such as adding a splash of hot sauce to ketchup. Many barbecue sauces are sweet and ketchupy, so you could try a bridge to barbecue sauce if you like ketchup.

- **Make a condiment caddy with things you enjoy or have enjoyed in the past.** Set it up neatly so you can leave it out at meal and snack time. Look for a makeup organizer or shower caddy in which you keep a variety of choices such as a small container of crunchy wonton strips, crumbled pretzels, hot sauce, or sprinkles.

A sensory "avoider" may describe someone with sensory issues who finds certain foods overwhelming: too crunchy, too sharp, too intense, just too everything. It's like that amplifier that's always at 11. If that describes you, you may prefer bland and smooth foods, room-temperature foods and few spices.

Sensory "seekers" tend to need more input to register sensations. Sensory seekers may prefer hot sauce, bubbly drinks, crunchy wasabi peas, or ice chips.

Some people are a little of both. Knowing what you prefer helps you think of other similar foods you can try.

some sample bridges

- Try a different brand of chicken nuggets.

- Go from fried chicken to fried fish.

- If you like Rice Chex, try a different flavor of Chex cereal.

- Try new flavors of ice cream (you can even "fade" one flavor into the next by mixing a small amount of a new flavor into one you like.)

- Add small amounts of new fruits to a smoothie you like.

- Add small amounts of a new food to something you already eat, similar to how Jenny did with cheese in the previous example. Options include a tiny taste of well-cooked fish on a piece of bread or a tortilla chip dipped in black bean salsa.

- If you like cheese pizza, try a new brand or add a topping.

You might want to start really small. Marsha Dunn-Klein is an occupational therapist who literally co-wrote the textbook on the development of feeding skills in kids. She shares one of her signature strategies she has used with all ages: crumbs. "Crumbs help bridge from dry cracker snack crumbs to wetter crumbs. You can make crumbs with familiar dry foods and then gradually grade to a crumb with more moisture, such as dry toast or a breakfast bar. At your own pace, you can work toward corn muffin crumbs, other bread crumbs, waffle crumbs, and gradually waffle pieces! Grated cheeses are also a moister crumb choice. You might prefer less "snacky" foods such as freeze-dried peas, corn, or fruits that crumble nicely between fingers or in a coffee-bean grinder. Cheese can be finely shredded, 'crumbs' or powdered, as in Parmesan cheese, and you can find them in many varieties. Seeds such as sesame, flax seeds, or chia seeds add still another texture with some nutritional benefits. If you like crunchy but don't eat fruits or veggies, you can dip into freeze-dried fruit or veggie crumbs and add a whole new food group."

You can make crumbs with your fingers, a food processor, the back of a spoon, or in a plastic bag using a rolling pin or meat mallet. You can pick crumbs up with your finger and lick them off or mix them into yogurt or other foods, and you can try flavors from mild (Rice Krispies) to more bold (teriyaki chips or wasabi dried peas). As Dunn-Klein says, "Your first taste doesn't have to be a big bite with your nose plugged and chased down with water!"

check in

How is the phrase "Part of me feels…" from Chapter 8 working out? This phrase can reframe anxiety and help you feel less overwhelmed. If you've forgotten, remind yourself to try this phrase over the next few days. You can even put a sticky note on your mirror that says, "Part of me feels…", or an alert on your phone.

_____

_____

notes

_____

_____

_____

_____

_____

_____

_____

34
offer yourself many opportunities

You may have heard that it takes "ten tries" to learn to like a new food. It tends to take a persistently selective eater much longer. You may be surprised to find you like some foods on the first try (or at least that you don't *dislike* them) or that they are different than you imagined in terms of taste or texture. This process takes *lots* of patience. Be kind to yourself! Offering yourself frequent opportunities and different ways to try flavors and textures increases the odds you will find something you like—or can learn to like—over time.

take advantage of free samples

Sometimes being away from meals or the kitchen table is the most relaxed way to try new foods; there just isn't the same expectation. You might feel braver eating out with a friend, or curious to try samples at a farmer's market or grocery store while browsing.

Go to Costco, Sam's Club, Central Market, Trader Joe's, Whole Foods or other stores when they are offering samples. If something looks good, go for it! If you're not sure, walk around the entire store and just look at all the samples first. Give yourself permission not to try any, but if you feel up to it, choose one new food to try on the second time around. Go alone or with a supportive friend.

Do you think you'd rather go alone or with a friend? _____

Where can you go to find samples? _____

Bring a paper napkin with you to the store. As with trying any new food, you can discreetly spit it out into a napkin if you don't like it. Consider bringing a favorite drink with you to wash it down, or a favored piece of candy or gum to clear any unexpected tastes.

If you like something, buy it and bring it home. Consider adding it as an eating opportunity (EO) during the following few days, but remember—you don't have to eat it! If possible, buy a small amount at first. Buying large quantities of a new food can make you feel as though you have to eat it all. You don't!

Journal your thoughts about the samples you tried at the store. Or don't. You're getting the hang of this by now. If you feel dread pulling out that journal, skip it. If you feel curious and want to write some notes, go for it!

_____

_____

_____

_____

_____

Check out the bulk bin at your local co-op or grocer. Choose three familiar items (or one or two) the first time and bag up a small amount. Usually you have to label the bag with a tag and write the number from the matching bin. Take time to examine your options, reading the ingredients to see if the food might be salty or sweet. Use your preferred food characteristics to help you think of what to try if you feel stuck; dried mango strips might be a good fit if you like the texture of fruit leather, or crunchy wasabi peas might appeal if you like spicy and crunchy foods. (Remember the process called *food chaining, bridging,* or *stretching* that uses a familiar and liked food as a starting point to new foods?)

You might need to ask a parent, friend, or older sibling to take you to the store or buy the foods for you if you don't earn your own money. You can review Chapters 21 and 39 for how to ask family members for help if your family isn't yet on board. If you don't have access to shops with bulk foods, look for other opportunities to sample foods, from parties to potlucks at sporting events or places of worship.

Write down which three items you chose:

1. _____

2. _____

3. _____

Next time you shop, buy something new from the bulk section, even if you don't eat it.

What did you pick? _____

Put a small portion of the foods out as a snack (alongside foods you eat so you don't go hungry) with no expectation to eat it. How does that feel?

_____

_____

If you are ready, give the food a try. Remember, you can spit it out. How did it go?

_____

_____

If you prefer, incorporate the bulk food items into your mindful eating explorations (from Chapter 31) and see if the foods match your expectations. Describe the texture and flavor. Were there any surprises?

_____

_____

_____

If the new food wasn't unpleasant, see if you can try it again. You may discover after a few tries that you've added a new food to your menu.

> You may have heard the expression that a particular food is "an acquired taste." Many widely enjoyed foods are quite bitter, such as coffee and beer. Most people don't like these foods right away. You could try saying, **"I don't like that yet,"** and give foods several tries. Clearly, there are foods you won't like, even after many exposures, but sometimes it takes many tries to become familiar with, and then to enjoy, eating certain foods. Ellyn Satter, a renowned childhood feeding expert, calls this natural process in childhood "sneaking up on" new foods. You can sneak up on new foods too, at your own pace.

See if you can come up with five (or more!) different preparations to try a new food—blueberries, for example.

1. _____   4. _____

2. _____   5. _____

3. _____   6. _____

Do any of the above options sound good? Are they similar to a food or texture you already enjoy?

_____

_____

_____

If so, try to offer the new food as an option to yourself at meal and snack times, or during a mindful eating session. **Remember, you don't have to eat or even taste anything, but if it is never in front of you as an option, then you don't even have the opportunity.**

Go on Pinterest and search "blueberries" (or whichever food you chose) and research other ways to try them. See if any of those ideas look good to you.

Follow up: look back at the foods you like and why from page 105. If you like crunchy foods, the following are some ideas for our blueberries example: freeze-dried, frozen, topped with crunchy toppings such as granola or chopped nuts. If you prefer smooth textures, you can try smoothies, jam, yogurt, or ice-cream flavors.

If you like pancakes, try blending blueberries in a food processor and mix them into the batter, put whole or halved blueberries in a few pancakes, or keep them separate to try on top. You can also try blueberries in muffins or other baked goods.

Now try this exercise again with a food in your "eat now and enjoy" column from your food preferences list (Appendix I). Write down as many different ways as you can that you could offer this food to yourself. Then **circle** the ways that line up with your preferred textures, flavor, temperature etc.

_____

_____

_____

Select two foods from your "interested in trying" column. Think of ways to offer yourself these more challenging foods that share characteristics with your preferred foods.

Food: _____

Different ways to try it:

_____

_____

_____

Food: _____

Different ways to try it:

_____

_____

_____

When you feel ready, choose one food and preparation and either try a mindful eating exploration with it (Chapter 31) or review the bridging to new foods list (Chapter 33) for ideas. Did you try it? What did you learn?

_____

_____

_____

Try a new presentation of an accepted food: you might prefer carrots sliced in thin circles over carrot sticks, or celery chopped finely and cooked until soft in a soup over the crunch of a celery stick.

Give yourself many opportunities: many ways, many times.

Multiply your opportunities. Go to a buffet with your support person. (I know! We love buffets!) On your plate, put a small taste of three items that look appealing, or at least don't look off-putting. Small amounts are less threatening. Take a favorite cracker or bread (or anything that works for you) and maybe dip it into a sauce or soup. You can stop there until you feel ready, then touch the soup or sauce to your lip.

What did you choose?

1. _____

2. _____

3. _____

How does a buffet versus ordering off a menu feel in terms of trying something new?

_____

_____

Were you surprised by anything you put on your plate, tried, or didn't try?

_____

_____

How did your support person do? What did they do that helped?

_____

_____

What might have helped you even more?

_____

_____

Do you feel you could talk to your support person about the experience? _____

> Double your options without more work. If you are cooking a dish with vegetables
> at home, include a small bowl of the same vegetables, only raw, on the table.
> You may prefer the crunch of a raw sugar snap pea over it sautéed in a little olive
> oil and salt.

notes

_____

_____

_____

_____

_____

_____

_____

_____

_____

_____

35

take control with cooking and baking skills

Being able to feed yourself is a life skill with many benefits, including saving money, allowing you to control what you eat, and exploring at your own pace.

- Look into taking a cooking class. You could talk to or email the instructor ahead of time to make sure you don't have to eat the food.

- Check out "cooking for beginners" tutorials online and give cooking a try, even if you choose not to eat the food. If you have never cooked, start with making familiar boxed and prepared foods. Start with something simple. Follow the directions closely.

- Many selective eaters enjoy sweeter foods or baked goods. Baking can be a great place to become familiar with the kitchen and the skills involved in cooking. Start with something you already like to eat. There is even some research that baking can help with anxiety! Bake cookies, cupcakes, or muffins. Try a new flavor of familiar baked foods.

Learning to bake or cook is as much about "failure" as anything. Check out "nailed it" cooking and baking memes online for some inspiration. Don't be afraid to make mistakes when cooking; it's part of the process. We both cook often and find that only about one in four new recipes we try will make it into a regular rotation. Start slow, and don't give up!

check in

Go back to the mindful eating exercises in Chapter 31. If exploring foods from the "eat now but don't enjoy" list wasn't too challenging, choose a few more foods off that same list or the next row over. Pick a food that is a little harder or that you are less excited about trying. Always check in with your body to see if it is too much. Consider doing these exercises with a support or discovery partner. Choose two foods and set aside two separate times to explore them.

What did you pick? _____

Why? _____

_____

When are you planning to explore them? _____

What did you learn? _____

_____

_____

notes

_____

_____

_____

_____

_____

_____

_____

_____

_____

_____

_____

_____

_____

36
reward yourself

Celebrate successes in a meaningful way *for you*. Often, gaining comfort around new foods and skills is reward enough. Remember to look for those early signs of improvement and reward yourself for those—if you want to! In the past, you may have been rewarded for trying foods, which may not have helped. Some studies suggest that rewarding kids for eating makes them like the foods even less! Studies on adults in the workplace show the same thing: Rewarding adults to encourage certain behaviors can backfire. If rewards actually make you feel worse ("I didn't try it, now I don't get a reward!") skip them.

◆

If, however, you *want* to celebrate your progress, **figure out what reward motivates you or reinforces good feelings.** The following are some ideas:

- A new song on iTunes, a new app, or a game upgrade.

- Positive self-talk and encouragement.

- Self-kindness on days of stress or little progress: "Today I was stressed about the test, so I took care of myself by remembering to make time for dinner with foods I like."

- Put some money away for a special event such as a concert or trip.

- Share your successes with your support person. If you feel safe including your parents in rewards and excitement about progress, let them know! If you think doing so might result in more attention on your eating (which can create expectations and pressure), you don't have to tell them. Your supportive friend may be more able to give you a "way to go!" that doesn't carry all the baggage that might come along with telling your parents.

- List some ideas for rewards, either as motivation to cook or schedule meals, or just to make yourself feel good!

_____

_____

_____

notes

37
deal with smells

For some selective eaters—particularly those who have sensory issues—strong smells (or even not-so-strong smells) can kill appetite and even trigger gagging in some people. In addition, smells and emotions are closely linked. A certain smell can bring you right back to a place or time and all the feelings that come with that memory. Cinnamon rolls may remind you of your grandma, with the smell of cinnamon triggering real feelings of relaxation and closeness.

When smells have been associated with *bad* memories, such as stressful feeding therapy or being made to eat a few bites of that yam dish at Thanksgiving, they can be an equally powerful trigger of stress and negative emotions. It may take a bit of sleuthing to determine if you are reacting to a smell itself, a memory associated with a smell, or both.

> You might discover that when you trust you don't have to try a food or interact with it, the smell of that food might not bother you as much. Stay curious!

If you have discovered that smells are an obstacle to your enjoyment of eating and certain foods, the following are some ideas for dealing with strong-smelling food.

- **Use a breeze.** Point a small fan toward the strong-smelling foods and away from your seat, use it while you are cooking, or open a window.

- **Keep your distance.** Move the dining table farther away from the kitchen, serve any strong-smelling foods in the kitchen instead of the table, or put the foods farthest away from you at the table. No need to make a fuss; just put them there in a matter-of-fact way.

- **Cover your nose.** Fit a bandanna over your nose or use a nose plug while cooking, prepping or eating in private. You might not want to use this technique at a restaurant!

- **Practice what to say if someone sits near you with a smelly food.** "I'm sensitive to the smell of fish. Nothing against you, but I'm going to switch seats."

◆

Try smell "training." If you want to check out the smell of a food or see if it bothers you, instead of just sticking your nose right up to the food, put your nose about six inches away and use your hand like a fan to waft some of the smells toward your nose. Move the food closer if it doesn't bother you too much.

What foods did you choose?

_____

What did you observe?

_____

_____

_____

With a smell that used to bother you, taking a small whiff is enough. You don't have to get closer or sniff deeply to the point that it is upsetting. Over time, keep giving the food a sniff, and you might find the smell no longer bothers you. If this exercise feels like too much attention to the process, or you dread doing it, try something else.

When something smells okay or even good, pause and try to describe why you enjoy it. Focus on food, drinks or cooking smells, but be curious even around flowers, candles, creams or essential oils.

_____

_____

Does it bring back a positive memory?

_____

_____

Does it remind you of another smell or a food you enjoy? Maybe mint tea, lemon, or chocolate cake?

_____

_____

38
deal with nausea

Some selective eaters feel nauseated at times. This may be caused by anxiety or, rarely, a medical condition. If you feel nausea, be sure you have talked with a doctor to rule out underlying medical causes. Nausea and anxiety are often involved in a vicious cycle. Feeling anxious that you might throw up can *cause* nausea! (Review steps to help manage anxiety in Chapter 20.)

The following are some techniques to combat nausea:

- **Breathe deeply.** Take your mind off the feelings by counting to four as you breathe in, hold for four, and count to four as you exhale.

- **Try long deep breaths in** and slowly exhale through pursed lips like you are blowing out a candle.

- **Sigh loudly** three times in a row. Raise your shoulders as you prepare with a deep breath and lower your shoulders as you sigh.

- **Spit food out** discreetly into a napkin if you think you might gag.

- **Plan to chew right away.** Place the food on your side molars and begin chewing, instead of placing the food on your tongue.

- **Sing** a favorite song.

- **Press on the acupressure point** for nausea. Look up the P 6 acupressure point online: https://explore im.ucla.edu/self-care/acupressure-point-p6.

- **Wear a wristband** for nausea, available online or at pharmacies.

- **Sniff a drop of peppermint essential oil** on a cotton ball or on the back of your hand (if you apply essential oils to your skin, be sure they are diluted and test for a reaction).

- **Sip ginger tea** or ginger ale.

- **Avoid caffeine.**

- **Time your sleeping and exercising.** Don't lie down or exercise right after a meal, and try to eat your last meal about two hours before bedtime.

- **Cut out bubbly drinks** to help with occasional heartburn or vague discomfort.

- **Medications** might help. Talk to your doctor.

notes

39
help others *help you*

Eating with family can be difficult, whether it's every day or only on visits home. Holiday meals are particularly stressful and frequently spoiled by comments such as, "I thought you'd grow out of your picky eating!" or your aunt advising you to put "something green" on your plate. Setting boundaries may be easier if you aren't living at home, but it can still be really hard.

◆

Write out a letter you might send to those close to you, or as notes for a discussion. Before you begin, set aside some time to flip back through this workbook for insights you learned about your process that you can share. The following are some ideas to get you started.

- Thank them for what they do well and the positive impact they have on your life.
- Share your goals and update them on the process if you want to. "I've decided I want to work on eating more variety, and here's what I've been working on so far…"
- Describe both helpful and unhelpful things others have done.
- Ask them to help you shop, cook, or give you space to explore your situation.
- Ask them to praise or not praise your efforts as you find helpful.
- Ask to eat with them, or without them. Let them know your needs will likely evolve over time, and if you need to eat alone for now, that your goal may be to eat family meals together when you are ready.
- Offer to cook them a meal if you aren't ready to sit with them and eat it yet.
- Ask them not to comment during meals and to allow you to place foods on your plate.
- If you want, ask them to make time for at least one family meal a week when you eat together with accepted foods available and avoid tough topics.
- Other things you can think of? _____

Is there anyone to whom you want to send this letter or email? _____

Write down what you hope to hear back.

_____

_____

_____

Plan ahead for how you might care for yourself if you don't get the response you were hoping for. Review Chapters 13 and 20 for self-nurturing strategies and consider telling your support people in advance that you are sending a letter and might need some support. Asking for help and being vulnerable is brave.

You could also share Appendix V, which contains concrete tips on how to support selective eaters.

notes

40
do you need professional help?

Eating disorders are incredibly complex. Sometimes selective eating can get mixed in with restrictive (eating too little) eating disorders, such as anorexia nervosa; avoidant restrictive food intake disorder (ARFID); disordered eating; or binge eating disorder, in which you might feel out of control with your eating. If you want to eat more variety but have not been able to with the exercises in this book, ask for professional help. If your feelings of anxiety feel overwhelming, ask for professional help.

We've shared some warning signs along the way and want to say again: If you struggle with body image, worry about your weight, or view being picky (even secretly) as a good thing so you won't gain weight, please talk with someone who can get you help, such as a parent, doctor, school counselor, or therapist. **If you are losing weight, passing out, or experience low energy, difficulty sleeping or concentrating, depression, anxiety, or other concerning symptoms, talk to your doctor right away.**

The SCOFF Quiz (Sick, Control, One, Fat, Food) is a screening tool for eating disorders. If you answer yes to any of these questions, please seek professional help.[1]

4. Do you make yourself **S**ick because you feel uncomfortably full?

5. Do you worry you have lost **C**ontrol over how much you eat?

6. Have you recently lost more than **O**ne stone (approximately 15 pounds) in a three-month period? (*Note: If your baseline weight is lower than average, a smaller weight loss could be concerning, too.*)

7. Do you believe yourself to be **F**at when others say you are too thin?

8. Would you say that **F**ood dominates your life?

For help, start with your primary care physician and see if they work with specialists in eating disorders near you. It can be difficult to find qualified help, let alone deal with insurance. You may also wish to contact local eating disorder specialists or clinics. The following are some websites that can help:

- **Eating Disorder Hope:** www.eatingdisorderhope.com

- **Something Fishy** (website on eating disorders): www.something-fishy.org

- **National Eating Disorder Association:** www.nationaleatingdisorders.org

- **National Eating Disorder Information Centre (NEDIC):** www.nedic.ca, or toll-free help line at 1-866-633-4220

[1]Morgan, J.F., et. al. "The SCOFF Questionnaire: A New Screening Tool for Eating Disorders." *Western Journal of Medicine,* 172(3):164-5, March 2000 (Accessed online 2017).

For more eating disorder resources, see our website at www.extremepickyeating.com/teenadultresources.

If you need help talking with parents and loved ones or with advocating for your needs, family therapy can prove helpful.

final words

Our hope is that this book has helped you feel less alone and more confident in who you are right now. While your eating doesn't define you, you can use skills and tools to help you eat in a way that makes you happier and healthier, able to live and love and dream, and to spend your time thinking about things other than food.

notes

notes

appendix I:
food preferences list

When filling out this list, be as specific as possible: include brands, restaurants, specific flavors, preparation details such as "crust off," etc. For example:

- McDonald's fries

- Regular Triscuit

- Grilled cheese sandwich with one American cheese slice, crust cut off

Consider using pencil so you can come back and move food entries from one box to another. If you want to print out a copy, this form is also available under Conquer Picky Eating resources at: www.extremepickyeating .com/teenadultresources.

The categories and lists in the left "food categories" column are meant to jog your memory and provide new foods to consider. To add any food you don't see on the list, use the blank spaces at the bottom or write them into a similar category. We know a few of you don't "enjoy" any foods you eat. If there are foods you can *tolerate*, put those in the first group, "eat now and enjoy." Do your best to make this table work for you.

The following is an example:

food categories	eat now and enjoy	eat now but don't enjoy	used to eat but do not eat now	interested in trying	can't imagine eating
fast foods: pizza, burgers, fries, chicken nuggets/ tenders	plain cheese Domino's®, room temp		plain cheese Little Caesars®	plain cheese Little Caesars®	mushroom pizza

Name: _____   Date: _____

Circle any condiments/dips/sauces/toppings you eat:

butter	yellow mustard	Miracle Whip	caramel sauce
margarine	Dijon mustard	rainbow sprinkles	peanut butter
ketchup	pickle relish	cinnamon sugar	melted chocolate
hot sauce	Sriracha	frosting	melted cheese sauce
ranch dressing	wasabi paste	Nutella	Parmesan cheese from
barbecue sauce	mayonnaise	hummus	Kraft can

Others _____

_____

_____

_____

food categories	eat now and enjoy	eat now but don't enjoy	used to eat but do not eat now	interested in trying	can't imagine eating
bread: pita, whole wheat, white, brand names, toasted, no crust					
breakfast breads: waffles, French toast, pancakes, from scratch or frozen, muffins					
bagels, English muffins					

food categories	eat now and enjoy	eat now but don't enjoy	used to eat but do not eat now	interested in trying	can't imagine eating
sandwiches: tortilla/wraps					
sandwiches: grilled, on soft white roll, plain, no crust, subs					
pasta: noodles, macaroni and cheese, elbow macaroni, shells, buttered spaghetti, with sauce, pasta salad, plain					
rice: brown, white					
cereal: cold cereal, dry or with milk; brand; warm cereals, including oatmeal, Cream of Wheat, and any toppings					

food categories	eat now and enjoy	eat now but don't enjoy	used to eat but do not eat now	interested in trying	can't imagine eating
crackers: Ritz, Goldfish, Graham, Club, other brands					
food bars: granola, cereal bar, energy or fiber bar such as Clif bar					
crunchy snacks: potato chips kettle-cooked, Ruffles, Pringles, Cheetos, pretzels, cheese puffs					
desserts: cookies, cake, pie, cupcake, homemade, store-bought					
ice-cream or frozen treat flavors, brands					
candy: chocolates, red licorice, bars, hard candies					

food categories	eat now and enjoy	eat now but don't enjoy	used to eat but do not eat now	interested in trying	can't imagine eating
red meat: steak, ground beef, burger, beef hot dog, lamb chops					
pork: pork chops, ham (thin or thick slices), brats, hot dogs, bacon					
poultry: chicken, turkey, fried, roasted, nuggets, in soups					
deli meats: roast beef, bologna, turkey, salami					
seafood: breaded, fish sticks, shrimp, scallops, crab, tuna salad, plain tuna, baked or grilled					
mixed entrees: stews or casseroles, lasagna, soup					

food categories	eat now and enjoy	eat now but don't enjoy	used to eat but do not eat now	interested in trying	can't imagine eating
beans: bean soup, navy, black bean, refried, bean salsa					
tofu or other soy: edamame (soybeans), in the shell or without					
dips and salsas: Hummus, eggplant dip, yogurt dip, onion dip, tomato/corn/ fruit salsa					
protein or supplement drinks					
egg whites: scrambled, boiled, fried					
whole eggs: scrambled, fried, boiled, salad					

food categories	eat now and enjoy	eat now but don't enjoy	used to eat but do not eat now	interested in trying	can't imagine eating
nut or seed butters: peanut, cashew or sunflower butter, crunchy, creamy					
nuts: plain, roasted, honey-coated					
milk: lactose-free, flavored, whole milk or skim, in hot cocoa, Chai, or coffee drinks					
non-dairy milk: soy, almond, cashew, coconut, hemp					
yogurt: from cup, fruit-on-the-bottom, drinks, tubes, kefir yogurt drink					
soft cheeses: cottage cheese, sour cream, cream cheese					

food categories	eat now and enjoy	eat now but don't enjoy	used to eat but do not eat now	interested in trying	can't imagine eating
hard cheeses: cheddar, Swiss, melted, plain, grated, on chips					
smoothies: milk shakes, home-made, brands					
fruits (fresh or frozen): citrus, melon, berries, apples (with peel, without), bananas, pears					
fruits (dried, chewy): raisins, prunes, fruit leather					
fruits (freeze-dried crunchy): strawberries, blueberries					
fruits (canned): cocktail, mandarin oranges in syrup, half peaches, pineapple rings, chilled					

food categories	eat now and enjoy	eat now but don't enjoy	used to eat but do not eat now	interested in trying	can't imagine eating
vegetables (cooked): plain, with sauces, frozen (eat frozen or cooked), corn, mixed veggies, broccoli					
vegetables (raw or freeze-dried): plain, with dips, carrot sticks, grated carrot, jicama slices					
vegetables (canned): black olives, beans, peas, corn					
fast foods: pizza, burgers, fries, chicken nuggets/ tenders					
other:					
other:					

food categories	eat now and enjoy	eat now but don't enjoy	used to eat but do not eat now	interested in trying	can't imagine eating
other:					
other:					
other:					
other:					
other:					
other:					

appendix II:
food journal

Date: _____

FOOD JOURNAL

Time of day	Food(s) and/or beverage(s) offered	Notes

notes

appendix III:
considering weight

Throughout this workbook, we have introduced ideas around wellness and health that rarely mention weight. A typical assumption claims you can only be healthy within a very narrow range of weight, in a slim body... but not *too* slim, and certainly not "overweight." The categories of "overweight, normal, and underweight" are relatively arbitrary, meaning those cutoffs have changed over time and don't take into account muscle mass, body type, or other factors. **Simply put, the number on the scale is not a reliable way to know anything meaningful about your health** (with the now-familiar exception and reminder that if you are losing or have lost weight or not growing appropriately, you need to work with a medical and therapy team). Even if you are only above the cutoff by half a pound from the "normal" range, the label implies that anything other than "normal" weight or BMI is bad.

While this is a controversial area, many experts, us included, believe healthy bodies come in a range of sizes. It doesn't mean we ignore weight; we just look at weight gain and growth patterns over time as part of a picture of overall health and wellness. One person who is 5'4" tall and weighs 115 pounds (a BMI of 19, which is considered on the low "normal" range) may be at a healthy weight for them, while another person at the same height and weight may not be. Some selective eaters with low appetite are naturally lean and small (looking at family members and a thorough review of growth charts from birth can help determine if genetics are at play). Other selective eaters with low appetite are smaller than nature intended and leaner than what is healthy for them. This is often evidenced by weight loss or data on growth charts such as a noticeable downward shift from a stable growth pattern, low energy or fatigue and, in some cases, lab tests confirming poor nutrient intake. A history of challenges around feeding and eating make low weight more likely to be problematic.

Weight divergence, which means up or down from an expected pattern, calls for further investigation, taking into account eating behaviors as well as medical, nutritional, financial, and emotional/societal factors.

There is a concept of a weight "set point," in which a person who is not trying to control their weight generally has a relatively stable weight over time, usually within a 10-15 pound weight range rather than a specific number on a scale. Genetics play a big role in this set point, along with other factors. When people try to gain or lose weight, the body initiates mechanisms (such as slowing metabolism or the rate at which energy is used) to try to get back to that set point range. This is a major reason why approximately 90% of people who succeed at losing weight will gain the weight back. When eating is not going well, weight is more likely to diverge from that set point, meaning it goes up or down and away from what nature intended. The set point can shift higher, meaning as weight is gained over time—perhaps due to dieting, stressors, or other challenges—the body becomes less likely to return to the earlier set point. Dieting and periods of not having enough food slow metabolism, which makes further weight gain more likely.

It can be hard to determine a person's healthy weight range if their eating has been difficult for many years, especially if this included their childhood, when growth and weight gain are expected to follow certain patterns. Again, a concern over low weight calls for careful and experienced expert attention.

Because healthy bodies come in a range of sizes, we encourage readers to focus on health-promoting behaviors and not the number on the scale. Focus on things you can control, review Chapters 13 and 20, and see our resources section online to learn more at: www.extremepickyeating.com/teenadultresources.

appendix IV:
general guidelines on
nutrition and meal planning

daily protein intake

Some days you may eat more, and some days less, than the recommended amount. Rough estimates of daily protein needs can be calculated as follows:

- 7-14 year olds need about .45 grams per pound of body weight
- 15-18 year old males need about .4 grams per pound of body weight
- Females older than 15 and males older than 18 need about .35 grams per pound of body weight

A sample equation:

For females 15 and older and males 18 and older:

_____ (your weight in pounds) X .35 = _____ (how many grams to roughly aim for)

grams of protein in some common foods

Milk, 1 cup = 8 grams

Cheese, 1 ounce = 6-8 grams

Greek yogurt, 1 cup = up to 18 grams
   (check label)

Nuts or nut butter, 2 Tbsp = 7 grams

Deli meat (such as turkey),
   one slice = 5-10 grams

Egg, 1 medium to large = 7 grams

Beans and lentils, ½ cup cooked = 7-10 grams

Fish/shellfish/shrimp, 1 ounce = 7 grams

Edamame, ½ cup = 14 grams (cooked soybeans)

Tofu, ½ cup = 20 grams

Veggies, ½ cup cooked = 1-3 grams

Grains ½ cup cooked = 2-4 grams

Bread, 1 slice = 2-4 grams

Oats, ½ cup = 2-4 grams

Egg noodles, 1 cup = 7 grams

White pasta, 1 cup = 7-8 grams

Extra-protein pasta, ½ cup cooked = 10 grams

iron

Good food sources of iron include: beef, chicken, turkey, pork, shellfish, liver, canned sardines, soybeans (edamame or tofu), dark leafy greens, egg yolks, grains, beans, lentils, dried fruits, pumpkin seeds, baked potatoes, enriched breads, fortified cereals (look for 10% or more daily iron needs), brown and enriched rice, cashews, sunflower and sesame seeds, and enriched drinks such as almond and soy milk.

Vitamin C helps the body absorb iron from eggs and plant foods more efficiently. Try pairing iron-rich foods with these sources of Vitamin C: oranges, lemons, kiwi, strawberries, broccoli, bell peppers, sweet potatoes, and tomatoes. If none of these foods are on your accepted list, see if you can find a supplement to take with an iron-rich food. Vitamin C comes in hard candies and even lollipops.

meal planning tips

For clarity, we include a few paragraphs from Chapter 26 with additional ideas to help balance nutrition and offer satisfying eating opportunities (EOs).

When building a meal or snack, there are two equally acceptable approaches you can choose from. One way is to think of foods in terms of four basic "food groups," which include grains/starch, dairy, fruits and veggies, and meat/meat substitute. Or you can use the "macro" (main) nutrient building blocks of carbohydrate/starch, fat, protein, and fiber (generally in fruits and veggies). If you don't or can't eat dairy, thinking in terms of macronutrients may make it easier to cover your nutrition bases. Go with whichever approach you are most comfortable with.

For meals and snacks to last until the next EO, aim to include an option covering each macro nutrient if you can, or from each food group. It's okay to have more than one choice from a food or macronutrient group, or to have some EOs that don't cover all the bases.

We often ask clients to pick one filling and accepted food around which to build meals/snacks. For example, you could start with chicken nuggets which are a meat and provide fat and protein. You might then look at your list of preferred foods for ideas to add a fruit and/or vegetable and chose one or more. Adding an accepted carb/starch is another filling option. A snack could build on pretzels and go with 2% chocolate milk to round out nutrition with protein and fat, and freeze-dried strawberries from the fruit category add fiber. These are combinations that help keep energy up until the next EO.

Writing the menu helps you imagine options, whether or not you stick to it closely. This is a skill that takes time to develop. You might plan a menu—but be prepared for life to happen! Making changes, relying on safe foods, or eating out are all options, and giving yourself permission to be imperfect increases your odds of success.

Planning menus is a task most adults we know struggle with. You might find that a shopping and menu app works for you or you might prefer a notepad on the kitchen counter. If you see friends or family who do this well, see if they will share their techniques. See www.extremepickyeating.com/teenadultresources for meal-planning resources.

appendix V:
how to help your teen or
young adult conquer picky eating

The following letter from Skye Van Zetten, a parent of a teen with selective eating, draws on her experience supporting thousands of parents of children with extreme picky eating. We hope her insights will help you help your child.

Dear Parent,

Being the parent of a young teen who has struggled with food for most of their life is an isolating experience. I can think of few things that are more painful than feeling unable to nourish your child with food. Over the years, I've learned that it hurts just as much to be that child who cannot please his parents with his eating. This dynamic is responsible for endless mealtime battles where nobody emerges victorious.

While that immediate connection around the kitchen table is often spoiled with eating challenges, I've also come to understand that food is symbolic of connection, demonstrated worldwide through parents who are eager to pass along fond memories of sharing food in celebration with their children. When children resist meals that have been part of family traditions, sometimes for several generations, there is often a sense that the connection between one's ancestors and the youngest generation has been somehow severed. There is almost always a sense of loss.

While there are few statistics on picky eating, researchers estimate that about one in four children are picky eaters, and about half of this group will struggle with food acceptance in some way beyond childhood. In the United States alone, approximately 1 to 3 million 12-18 year olds are adversely affected by the sensory characteristics of food. At extremes, the number of foods some teens and adults are able to eat amount to two dozen items or less.

My worry and my stress about my son's eating did nothing to make him more willing to expand his food preferences. It did, however, motivate me to read and learn as much as I could about something even the Internet had never heard of. My search for information led me to the authors of this book, and their kind and gentle wisdom has been influential in my ability to nurture a more functional relationship around food with my son, and an environment that supports his eating ability. I decided to pay my gratitude forward through an online support group for parents (facebook.

com/groups/MealtimeHostage). To date, over seven thousand families around the world have discovered how to nurture strong family connections through positive mealtime experiences, and a healthier relationship with food using many of the same techniques included in this book.

Your teen's diet is limited to a short list of foods because of strong preferences and dislikes for taste, texture, and temperature. The thought of trying unfamiliar food is as foreign to them as eating the bark of a tree is to you. Where we can come together on common ground is with understanding that everyone has food they don't like, and everyone is entitled to the privilege of discovering for themselves which foods are enjoyable to eat and which foods are not. Your job as a parent is not to convince your teen to like the same food as you do, but to grant your teen permission to develop their own relationship with food on their own terms and in their own time. This doesn't mean you will throw your arms up in defeat; quite the contrary, because your teen still depends on you to provide them with opportunities for eating. You are the metaphorical vehicle that will guide your teen on their journey into new food experiences; you just have to let them drive.

How does a parent change their relationship around food with their teen? You might start by reading this book together and understanding that your teen will do the best with eating they are capable of. Some teens might prefer working through this book on their own, coming to you when they are ready. While your history with food may look different than your teen's future, it helps to accept that your teen wants the same thing for himself that you want for him... a healthy relationship with food.

It also helps to understand that your teen's journey will be an emotional ride for you. After all, this is your child and their future is full of your hopes for their success and well-being. It will be difficult, but necessary, to put your emotions aside while your teen practices the skills they need to be successful with food and with eating in social situations.

The journey your teen is about to take with food is their own. This book will provide valuable tools to help them navigate along the way to a place with eating you have hoped they would eventually reach. Trust your teen to find his or her own way.

Skye Van Zetten

how to help your teen or young adult conquer picky eating

Your teen or young adult is on a journey of discovery around their eating. You and your family may have a long history of struggle, worry, and conflict over food. As your child gets older your role has changed, from infancy when you provided all the food and made all the choices, to now, when your support is still important but in different ways.

Read through the exercises in the book. Get a sense of how complicated and challenging eating can be. Possibly you have struggled with your own eating. Perhaps you can join your child in some of the exercises, if they are open to it, or do them on your own. Parenting a teen or young adult is a tricky dance. You are needed, but they are also becoming independent and thriving adults. The following are some ways you can help, and you and your child may come up with others! Try to listen and remain open to new ideas.

- Try not to judge or criticize how your child eats right now.
- Work on being good company at meals. Focus on connecting with your child rather than on what or how much she eats.
- Be supportive around shopping for and cooking meals. Ask your child how you can help, then try to listen; perhaps a ride to the grocery store to pick out foods or a trip to Costco to sample items.
- Try not to comment or ask questions during their discovery process. Sometimes this can feel like pressure to your child. You can even ask, "Do you want me to ask questions, or would you like to wait and keep me posted?"
- Use phrases such as, "If you ever want to talk about this, I'm here," "How can I be helpful to you?" or "Would it help if I…?"
- Cheerleading their successes may feel like pressure, because they may not want to disappoint you the next time.
- If you think your child needs to work with a professional, help them identify resources and then support that process as best you can. (See Chapter 40 for red flags and resources on when to seek help.)
- Let them know you love them unconditionally. They may feel as though they disappoint you with their eating.
- Find ways to spend time together that don't involve food.
- When eating together, try to have at least one food you know your child can eat.
- If you are cooking or in charge of meals, consider your child's preferences. For example, make a mild chili and serve hot sauce on the side for those who like more spice. Serve a side they enjoy such as rice, corn bread, or rolls.
- Be patient with this process. It can take a long time to build a positive relationship with food.

If you or your child find it difficult to work through some parts of the workbook, please see the references section on our website at extremepickyeating.com for various levels of help to delve deeper into topics of disordered eating, body positivity, weight diversity, eating competence, and clinical eating disorders.

Also available as a PDF on our website www.extremepickyeating.com/teenadultresources if you wish to print this page of tips for family and friends.

notes

appendix VI
paying for food

If you find you are unable to afford to nourish yourself regularly with the foods you would like to eat, please reach out for assistance. High school students may qualify for free or reduced breakfast and lunch. Community college or university programs should offer information on housing and food assistance. There are federal (across the U.S.) and state-level programs that can help.

- SNAP Supplemental Nutrition Assistance Program: www.fns.usda.gov/snap/supplemental-nutrition-assistance-program-snap

- If you are pregnant, breastfeeding or postpartum, you and your child may qualify for assistance. https://www.fns.usda.gov/wic/women-infants-and-children-wic

There are also many budget-friendly cooking resources available at the library and online.

CPSIA information can be obtained
at www.ICGtesting.com
Printed in the USA
LVHW061526031019
633101LV00001B/27/P